Body

LANGUAGE

GORDON R. WAINWRIGHT

TEACH YOURSELF BOOKS

For UK order queries: please contact Bookpoint Ltd, 78 Milton Park, Abingdon, Oxon
OX14 4TD. Telephone: (44) 01235 400414, Fax: (44) 01235 400454. Lines are open from
9.00–6.00, Monday to Saturday, with a 24 hour message answering service.
Email address: orders@bookpoint.co.uk

For USA & Canada order queries: please contact NTC/Contemporary Publishing, 4255
West Touhy Avenue, Lincolnwood, Illinois 60646–1975, USA. Telephone: (847) 679 5500,
Fax: (847) 679 2494.

Long renowned as the authoritative source for self-guided learning – with more than 40
million copies sold worldwide – the *Teach Yourself* series includes over 200 titles in the
fields of languages, crafts, hobbies, business and education.

British Library Cataloguing in Publication Data
A catalogue record for this title is available from The British Library.

Library of Congress Catalog Card Number: On file

First published in UK 1985 by Hodder Headline Plc, 338 Euston Road, London, NW1 3BH.
This second edition published 1999.

First published in US 1985 by NTC/Contemporary Publishing, 4255 West Touhy Avenue,
Lincolnwood (Chicago), Illinois 60646–1975 USA. This second edition published 1999.

The 'Teach Yourself' name and logo are registered trade marks of Hodder & Stoughton Ltd.

Copyright © Gordon R. Wainwright 1985, 1999

Typeset by Transet Limited, Coventry, England.
Printed in Great Britain for Hodder & Stoughton Educational, a division of Hodder
Headline Plc, 338 Euston Road, London NW1 3BH by Cox & Wyman Ltd, Reading,
Berkshire.

Impression number   10 9 8 7 6 5
Year   2005 2004 2003 2002 2001 2000

CONTENTS

INTRODUCING BODY LANGUAGE

In this book you will learn a language which everybody knows already. This is the language of the body. Every time we talk to someone else the body supplements what we say with dozens of small gestures, eye movements, changes in posture and facial expression. The fact that everybody knows this language already will not prevent you from learning to 'speak' it more effectively. Hence the reason for this book.

Most people do not realize just how much they use this unspoken language every time they communicate with another person. They use it unconsciously. And so do you. It may be that you, too, do not realize it is possible to use body language more effectively. This book will prove otherwise. If you read it carefully and put its guidance into practice, especially through the exercises and experiments it contains, you will find yourself becoming more skilled in the use of body language. And also more skilled in understanding other people's use of it.

In the last twenty years, a great deal of research has been carried out in non-verbal communication. Workers from the various disciplines of psychology, sociology, anthropology and linguistics have studied aspects of human behaviour which appear to have a communicative function. A number of subdisciplines have sprung up – kinesics, proxemics and paralinguistics, for instance – to provide umbrellas under which various kinds of research have been undertaken. The result is that we now know a good deal more than we did about human interaction at the micro level. In many cases, what was intuitively felt to be true on the basis of common sense has been confirmed, but in others it has not. The purpose here is to explore this rapidly developing field to discover what has been learned and to assess the practical implications and applications of this new knowledge. We have tended in the past to view communication between people as almost exclusively a matter of using language. It is time we took more serious account of the impact of non-verbal factors in face-to-face interaction.

This book sets out to explain what is known from research findings about the skills and techniques of body language such as bodily contact, proximity, orientation, facial expressions, non-verbal aspects of speech, and so on. It examines how this knowledge is applied in a variety of contexts and also how it may be applied to better effect. The remainder of this introduction will, therefore, outline briefly, but in a little more detail than is possible in a table of contents, the topics that you can expect to encounter later. Hopefully, this will help to convince you that it will be worth your while to persevere with your reading of the book and perhaps also to participate in some of the practical exercises and experiments which are suggested at the end of each chapter. In the use of body language, as in many other fields, at least as much may be learned from doing as from reading about what others do. But the main hope in providing this outline is that, by the time you reach the end of this introduction, you will have a clearer idea of what is meant by the term 'body language', what kinds of behaviour it includes and also, from their omission, what kinds of behaviour it is *not* meant to include.

Eye contact and direction of gaze are considered in Chapter 1. They are arguably the most potent means of non-verbal communication we possess. Eye contact maintained a fraction of a second longer than the individual looked at considers appropriate can lead to a reaction of physical aggression or, in another context, be taken as an indication of sexual attraction. We have to be careful what we are doing with our eyes.

Chapter 2 deals with facial expressions, including smiling. The smile is one of the few universals in body language, as is the 'eyebrow flash' of recognition and greeting. Our faces may not always be our fortunes, but they are certainly where some of the most powerful non-verbal signals originate.

Head movements and head nods, though strictly speaking gestures, are considered separately in Chapter 3. Their role in social interaction is explained and the importance of head nods when listening to others is discussed.

Gestures and body movements provide the focal point for Chapter 4. It is in this area that many researchers have looked for evidence of the existence of a body language with strict rules like spoken languages, so far without success. However, as we shall see, there are some indications that certain gestures in certain cultures have quite specific and fixed meanings and a number of gesture languages do exist, such as those used by deaf people, but there are many and obvious differences between these and the way gestures are used in normal everyday life.

Chapter 5 examines the role of posture and stance in body language. Until recently this was thought to be an area more suited to treatment in manuals of etiquette and deportment, but it is now being taken more seriously as an aspect of behaviour which can be rich in useful non-verbal signals. Posture can, for instance, be a good indicator of an individual's state of mind at the time at which communication is taking place.

In Chapter 6 we look at proximity and orientation. Like posture, orientation can tell us a good deal about individuals' attitudes both to those with whom they are communicating and to the nature, subject and setting of the communication. The concept of personal space is explored, together with territoriality in human behaviour. There is also a brief discussion of the concept of defensible space and its personal and social importance.

Chapter 7 deals with body contact and touching. The main distinction that is made between these two is one of intent, for the former carries the implication of accidental touching and the latter implies a deliberate act. But the difference is not a rigid one and it is perhaps only possible to distinguish the two on the basis of which part of the body is doing the touching; touching implies that the hands are being used to make the contact.

In Chapter 8, appearance and physique are discussed. Simple changes to these can have a significant effect upon an individual's ability to interact successfully with others.

Chapter 9 considers timing and synchronization as aspects of body language. The importance of time in Western culture gives it an important role in communication. How well we synchronize when talking with others can also be a major factor in successful interaction.

Chapter 10 considers the non-verbal aspects of speech. What we say can be considerably affected by our use, deliberate or unconscious, of pauses, 'ers', 'ums', changes in tone, pitch, pace and accent, to name but a few of the features that are more important than many people suppose.

Cultural differences in the use of body language are the focus of attention in Chapter 11. An attempt has been made here to highlight some of the more unusual, unexpected and significant differences, as well as to explore the general nature of cross-cultural variations in non-verbal behaviour.

Chapter 12 explores the role of body language in occupations such as nursing, teaching, television interviewing, business and other forms of contact with the public.

Chapter 13 considers its role in various situations encountered in everyday life, as well as in attempts to deceive others. A systematic approach to analyzing other people's body language during small talk is suggested.

In Chapter 14, attention moves to the part played by body language in establishing and maintaining relationships with the opposite sex. It considers how non-verbal behaviour can be used to make an individual appear more attractive with better self-presentation and impression management.

Chapter 15 considers the role of body language in personal development, with discussion of its role in such areas as counselling and the development of interactive skills. It examines how effective use of body language can contribute to personal growth and the exploitation of human development. In addition, the role of body language in the development of synergic relations (that is, those in which the outcome is greater than the sum of individual inputs) is explored, together with its role in establishing rapport, empathy and a sense of togetherness. It also suggests how non-verbal behaviour can be observed and recorded for analysis.

In the concluding chapter we review what has been learned and consider the limitations and advantages of body language as a means of communicating. Suggestions for further reading complete the book and should prove helpful to the reader who wishes to explore the subject further.

Part One
SKILLS AND TECHNIQUES

1 | EYE CONTACT

We begin improving our mastery of body language by looking at the eyes and at how they are used in the process of everyday face-to-face communication. We begin with the eyes because they are the most powerful means of communication we possess, after words (although sometimes a single glance can speak volumes, as they say). This power of the eyes is at its greatest, of course, when two people are looking at each other (which usually means looking at each others' eyes). This is usually called mutual gaze or, as we shall call it here, eye contact.

Why eye contact should be so powerful is not clear. Several writers on non-verbal communication (an alternative and more accurate term for body language) have speculated on the possible reasons. Some have suggested that, from the cradle, we find other people's eyes of compelling interest and will even respond to sets of circles that look like eyes because it is through the eyes that we first have contact with others. Some have suggested our response to eye contact is instinctive and connected with basic survival patterns, in that youngsters who could secure and retain eye contact, and therefore attention, stood the best chance of being fed and of having their other needs satisfied. Others have suggested that the significance of eye contact is learned and that, as we grow up, we quickly learn not to misbehave if an adult is watching us or we learn that certain kinds of look tell us that people like us (or dislike us).

Whatever the reasons, the power of eye contact in communication is clear and we shall give most of our attention here to considering the forms it takes, the uses it can be put to, and how we can use it more effectively. First of all, though, let us begin our study of eye contact with an exercise. It will be helpful, as you read through this book, if you can find the time to carry out the simple exercises and experiments described. In this way, you will learn better body language in the same way you would learn to improve any other language. Here is an exercise in eye contact for you to try as soon as a suitable opportunity presents itself. After it, we shall discuss the kind of results you might have expected. We shall do this in each chapter so that you will have plenty of opportunities to put the instruction offered into practice. You will find it helpful if, as you work through this book, you record your responses to the exercises in a notebook. Alternatively, if you have a cassette recorder, you may prefer to record them on tape. In this way, you will have something to refer to when you read through the Exercise Review which follows each major exercise. You will find that this increases the benefit you derive from your study of body language.

EXERCISE: WHAT ARE THEY LOOKING AT?

Next time you are in a public place, like a bar or a restaurant, observe the other people present as discreetly as you can. Note how they look at each other when they are talking. Note how long each period of eye contact is (no need to time it – just note whether the mutual glances are short or long). Do they spend all their time looking at each other or do they look around at the other people present? Do they spend much time looking at objects in the room? How do they react when someone enters or leaves? What kinds of people look at each other the most (and least) when they are talking? How do the patterns of eye contact of people sitting side by side differ from those of people sitting opposite each other? What else do you notice about patterns of eye contact?

If your discreet observations are noticed by others, it will be advisable to abandon them for a while. The reason for this is that people can react in unpredictable ways to being watched. Some become embarrassed, some will consider you some sort of eccentric, others may become irritable and even aggressive. You might like to speculate on why this should be so. What is it about being watched that should be so disturbing? Some of the possible reasons will be suggested in the next section, but you will find it useful to consider the problem first yourself before you read them.

Exercise review

So, what did you find out? If the observations you made were anything like typical (as indicated by the research studies on which this book is based), you will probably have noticed some of the following points:

1 When people are talking, they do not look at each other the whole time, but only in a series of glances.

2 In places like bars and restaurants, some time will be spent in looking at other people present, especially those who are attractive or who may be behaving oddly (e.g. drunks and those engaged in disputes with a waiter).

3 Unless the above criteria apply, little attention will be paid to staff members of the establishment and even confidential conversations will probably continue uninterrupted when staff are within earshot (the same usually happens in places like taxis and chauffeur-driven cars).

4 When people pay more attention to objects in the room and even to the decoration, it may signify that they are bored with the conversation, are newcomers to the place, or are so familiar with each other (e.g. those who have been married a long time) that little conversation is necessary (or possible).

5 Leaving or entering a room tends to attract attention. Many people who are a little embarrassed about walking alone into a bar or a restaurant tend to forget that this initial curiosity is typical and that it will cease as soon as someone else enters.

6 Those who are having an intimate, personal conversation may look at each other more and for longer than those who are not.

7 People sitting opposite each other will display more eye contact than those sitting side by side. If those sitting side by side desire more eye contact they will turn to face each other.

8 You will probably not have been conducting this

exercise for many minutes before someone has noticed what you are doing or is at least aware that you are not behaving normally.

Some of the possible reasons why people find it disturbing to be watched by someone else are:

1 The watcher may have the intention of harming them in some way.

2 Being watched makes you ask yourself why you are being watched, which makes you self-conscious and therefore undermines your self-confidence.

3 The watched may feel they ought to recognize the watcher and if they cannot this may disturb the pattern of their interaction with others.

4 They may think the watcher is sexually attracted to them and may not find him or her attractive, which would make them want to avoid eye contact. They would find this difficult, and therefore embarrassing or irritating, if the watcher continued watching.

5 They may be being rather silly, as people often are when with loved ones or friends, and may feel that the watching stranger will assume they are always like that. This might be a blow to their images of themselves as intelligent and sophisticated people.

6 They may take the watching as a sign that the watcher wants to join their group and group members often do not welcome newcomers as this affects the structure of the group. The smaller the group, the stronger this feeling may be (witness the popular proverb, 'Two's company, three's a crowd').

Eye grammar

Now that we have completed our first exercise, let us examine some of the forms eye contact can take and some of the rules which govern its use. Eye contact can be long lasting (as when two lovers gaze into each other's eyes) or it can be short (as when looking at someone we know does not like being stared at). It can be direct (a bold, full-frontal gaze) or indirect. It can be intermittent (the kind we use in conversation simply to check that the other person has understood us) or continuous (as in a stare).

There are rules about where we can look at each other and for how long. Try looking at someone's genital region or down a girl's low-cut dress and you will soon realize that you have broken a rule. Many people will find it embarrassing just to read that last sentence, let alone try it out, so rigid is the rule under all but the most exceptional circumstances.

Too much eye contact can be very unsettling for most people. Staring is usually considered impolite, at the very least. The only people who seem to be able to use a frank, open stare are young children, in whom it may even be regarded favourably as a sign of a healthy curiosity about the world.

It is nearly always tolerated in children, but some mothers (especially of middle-class backgrounds) may tell children of school age that it's rude to stare. It is almost never tolerated in adults and those who stare are often regarded as mentally deficient or socially dangerous and threatening in some way. A continuous stare is an easy way to unsettle or provoke someone.

Most of the rules of eye grammar (as is the case with all other forms of body language) are dependent on the context in which eye contact occurs. Some, however, are universal– that is to say they have similar applicability in any context, at any time, anywhere in the world (or almost anywhere). The main ones, according to Michael Argyle (see Further Reading at the back of the book) and other researchers, are:

1 Too much eye contact (as in staring or frequent glances at another person) is generally regarded as communicating superiority (or at least the sense of it), lack of respect, a threat or threatening attitude, and a wish to insult.

2 Too little eye contact is interpreted as not paying attention, being impolite, being insincere, showing dishonesty, or being shy.

3 Withdrawing eye contact by lowering the eyes is usually taken as a signal of submission.

4 A person will look at another a lot when:
- they are placed far apart
- they are discussing impersonal or easy topics
- they are interested in the other and their reactions
- they like or love the other person
- they are trying to dominate or influence the other
- they are extrovert
- they are dependent on the other and the other has been unresponsive.

5 A person will look at another very little when:
- they are placed close together
- they are discussing intimate or difficult topics
- they are not interested in the other's reactions
- they don't like the other person
- the other person is of higher status
- they are introverted
- they are suffering from one of certain forms of mental illness.

People will communicate with each other more effectively if their interaction contains the amount of eye contact they both find appropriate to the situation.

Uses of eye contact

A number of the uses that we make of eye contact have already been mentioned, but there are others. Broadly speaking, most of the uses can be grouped into six categories. We establish eye contact when we are:

1 Seeking information.
2 Showing attention and interest.
3 Inviting and controlling interaction.
4 Dominating, threatening and influencing others.
5 Providing feedback during speech.
6 Revealing attitudes.

Let us examine each of these categories a little more closely. The kind of information we acquire through eye contact consists of such things as clues about whether or not someone is telling us the truth (liars tend to avoid eye contact unless they are very brazen); whether someone likes us or not; whether the other person is paying attention to or understanding what we say; what a person's state of mind is (people who are depressed or introverted, for instance, tend to avoid eye contact); and whether a person recognizes us or not (here, eye contact will be used together with facial expression to arrive at a decision).

As soon as we look at someone, they know they have our attention. If we look at them for longer than a few seconds, they will infer that they also have our interest. Eye contact plays a vital role in one aspect of showing attention and interest – in sexual attraction. Consider the problem of indicating to a stranger that you are sexually attracted to her (or him) if you are unable (or too shy) to look at her. We shall consider the part played by all aspects of body language in sexual attraction in Chapter 14.

When we look at someone, we invite them to interact with us. If this interaction takes place, eye contact is then used in a number of ways to control the nature and duration of the interaction. It plays a major role in synchronizing what happens between two people.

Not only is there more looking at the other when listening than when speaking, but eye contact also signals the end of an utterance when one speaker is, as it were, handing the floor over to the other. When we greet people we not only look at them but also move our eyebrows up and down quickly once. This 'eyebrow flash' as it is called occurs world-wide in a variety of cultures as an indication of recognition and greeting (see Chapter 2). When eye contact is broken, another pattern is seen. Individuals habitually break gaze to left or to right – that is, when they look away, they look to something else to the right or the left of the speaker. There is some evidence to suggest that left breakers tend to be arts rather than science-trained and to be visualizers with strong imagination. Right breakers tend to be science-trained and to have less visual imagination. Further, if people are posed verbal questions they will tend to break gaze to the right and downwards; if they are asked spatial questions they will tend to break to the left and upwards, though this tendency is not as marked. Winking can also be used to control interaction to indicate that something is not to be taken seriously or to show a friendly attitude toward the other.

Long, unflickering looks are used by those who seek to dominate, threaten, intimidate or otherwise influence others. Many people do not like to feel dominated or threatened so that, if this kind of behaviour occurs in situations like negotiations or interviews, it can have an adverse effect on the outcome.

Feedback is important when people are speaking to each other. Speakers need to be reassured that others are listening and listeners need to feel that their attentiveness is appreciated and that speakers are talking to them rather than at them. Both sets of requirements can be met by the appropriate use of eye contact. The effects of eye contact in interpersonal communication are explored in the exercises at the end of this chapter.

Attitudes are often revealed by the willingness, or otherwise, of one person to provide another with opportunities for eye contact. People who like each other engage in more eye contact than those who do not. Aggression, an extreme form of dominance, may be signalled by prolonged eye contact – the phrase 'eyeball to eyeball confrontation' conveys what is involved here. Shame, embarrassment and sorrow are usually characterized by the deliberate avoidance of eye contact. Other emotions, too, have typical eye behaviour. When people are excited, their eyes tend to make rapid scanning movements. When they are afraid, their eyes appear to he frozen open, as if not to miss the slightest movement that may bring danger nearer. When people are angry, their eyes narrow, often into little more than slits. Sadness is expressed by looking downwards as well as by reducing eye contact, and this seems to happen almost universally.

Research into eye contact

It is not part of the purpose here to discuss research methods, and those who are interested in exploring the subject of eye contact in more detail should read *Gaze and Mutual Gaze* by Michael Argyle and Mark Cook (Cambridge University Press). But it is interesting to note that experiments have shown that people, especially children, will respond even to very simple drawings of eyes in much the same way as they respond to eyes themselves. Eye movements when perceiving stationary objects, or when reading, follow similar patterns to those used in the perception of people. There are cultural variations in eye contact, as we shall see in Chapter 11. A good deal of evidence has accumulated to indicate that greater eye contact leads to greater liking – you can actually come to like someone more by engaging in more eye contact with them.

There are considerable individual differences in the amounts and types of eye contact employed (as, for instance, between introverts and extroverts, or men and women) and there is the consequent need to note the context carefully before attempting too free an interpretation of the precise meaning of a particular pattern of eye contact. Patterns of eye contact change with certain kinds of mental illness and this may become a diagnostic tool in the future. Even when people are talking on the telephone, and therefore cannot see each other, eye movement patterns have many similarities with those in face-to-face communication.

In these and other areas, research into eye contact and eye movement behaviour is revealing that the communicative uses of the eyes are many and varied. The eyes are coming to be seen as much more than 'windows to the soul' and it will be useful at this point to consider some of the secrets of the eyes that we are only now beginning to learn.

What our pupils can teach us

Two intriguing facts about eye behaviour have been discovered in recent years. One is that when we see something interesting our pupils dilate. The other is that we like people with dilated pupils better than those with contracted pupils.

The first fact was the result of research carried out by Eckard Hess and reported in his book *The Tell-Tale Eye* (Van Nostrand Reinhold). In his experiments he showed people a set of five pictures: a baby, a mother and baby, a nude male, a nude female. and a landscape. He measured pupil responses to these pictures and found that men's pupils dilated most to the nude female (except for homosexuals, whose pupils dilated most to the male nude). Women's eyes dilated to the male nude, but dilated most to the mother and baby. His researches established that these pupil changes equated to people's interest in the various pictures.

Hess also showed people two pictures of the face of an attractive girl. The pictures were identical, but in one the pupils had been retouched to make them appear larger. Almost everyone asked thought the picture with the enlarged pupils was more attractive, but very few were able to say why. It seems, therefore, that while we respond to pupil changes, we are not aware of their effect on our responses at the conscious level (see Figure 1.1).

Pupil responses have also been used to measure attitudes towards various things, such as products advertised or political candidates: the more favourable the attitude, the more dilated the pupils. It is also possible to measure changes in attitude by measuring changes in pupil responses over time. Because pupil changes are not within our conscious control they provide a very reliable indication of interest, attraction and a number of different attitudes.

Figure 1.1 Both faces are smiling, but to most people the one on the left appears cold and insincere. What do you think?

Making better use of your eyes

How can we use the kind of information given in the last few pages to improve our use of this aspect of body language?

Firstly, we can become more observant. We can, without making it too obvious, pay a little more attention to where other people are looking and for how long. We can be particularly observant about any changes in pupil size. This can clearly be done only with people we are physically close to. We can note the amounts of eye contact that the different individuals we meet seem to prefer. And we can remember that we can often tell things about others' real thoughts and feelings from how and where they look that they would never think (or dare) to put into words.

Secondly, we can engage in more eye contact in order to promote greater liking of ourselves by others and to produce other positive responses.

Thirdly, we can remember that, on most occasions, a direct, open gaze is preferable to any hint of avoidance of eye contact or tendency to look quickly from one thing to another (which may he interpreted by others as shiftiness on our part).

Next, we can use all the information given above to increase our sensitivity to the kinds and amounts of eye contact appropriate in different contexts and avoid the extremes of staring or a total refusal to meet someone else's gaze.

We can develop positive attitudes towards other people since this will, quite unconsciously and without any effort, promote a more effective use of eye contact on our part. We can develop a more outgoing approach to other people for the same reason. If you like people and go out of your way to mix with them, this does seem, quite naturally, to produce a better use of eye contact.

Finally, we can use the information given in later chapters about other aspects of body language to enable us to integrate better use of eye contact into much more effective deployment of all our non-verbal and verbal communication skills.

What you should do now is to set some time aside over the next few days for practising the various uses of eye contact explored in the exercises which follow.

EXERCISES AND EXPERIMENTS

1 Look at me when I'm talking to you

With a person you know well, in an encounter, provide them with as much eye contact as you can without embarrassing them. Do they appear to take this as a signal that you want to carry on talking and prolong the encounter? You should find that they do.

2 Staring down

Stare at someone until they look away. Select someone you know well enough to conduct this experiment with but do not tell them about it in advance. Do not select a stranger as staring can easily be interpreted as aggressive behaviour and may well provoke aggression in return. Consider how you feel as you perform this experiment. Ask your subject how he or she felt during your staring. How long, approximately, was it before your subject looked away? If you are able to try this experiment with a number of people you should not only be able to explore in more detail your own feelings about staring but should also be able to collect quite a lot of useful information about the nature and effects of staring generally.

3 Look into my eyes

Select someone you know well and like very much. Persuade them to sit down with you and look into your eyes for about a minute. Then discuss what you both experienced during the experiment.

4 Does she/he like me?

Select an attractive stranger at a party, night club or other place where it is socially acceptable for strangers to approach and talk to each other. Try to decide from their eyes alone, as you chat casually (if the music allows), whether or not they like you. How does their willingness or otherwise to engage in eye contact affect your estimate of how much they like or dislike you? Observe other couples and try to assess the nature of their relationship from the amount and type of eye contact they engage in. How easy or difficult is it to select just one aspect of body language for observation in this way?

2 | FACIAL EXPRESSION

The study of facial expression has a long history. Charles Darwin, of *The Origin of Species* and *Voyage of the Beagle* fame, published the first serious scientific study, *Expression of the Emotions in Man and Animals*, in 1872. But physiognomy had exerted many pseudo-scientific minds before that. Several people tried to prove that facial appearance was a reliable indicator of a variety of human traits such as intelligence, criminality, emotional stability and even insanity. They failed, of course. It simply is not possible to use the face as a reliable predictor of very much at all. What can be done, however, as present research indicates, is to use facial expressions (that is, the face in movement rather than as a static object) as a means of gaining a better understanding of what others are communicating. In body language, the expressiveness of the face is second only to that of the eyes.

We gain a good deal of our information about people's emotional states from the expressions on their faces. Their attitudes towards us can be clearly seen, according to whether their expressions show pleasure or displeasure, interest or boredom, fear or anger.

Often the face is the first part of a person we look at and so expressions are used very much in greetings. One universal phenomenon we shall be considering in this chapter is the 'eyebrow flash', as one researcher has termed it. We shall see that facial expressions are very powerful in controlling the type and amount of communication which takes place between individuals.

We shall also see that we make personality and other judgements about people on the basis of what we see in their faces. People with attractive faces are often credited with having a number of other attributes – which they may or may not possess. Combined with the more effective use of the eyes, facial expressions can take us an important stage further in our quest for mastery of body language.

EXERCISE: SMILE IF IT KILLS YOU

Most of us will have seen, at one time or another, a small notice of the humorous kind that people working in offices and some places where the public are served often display, which states: 'Be difficult if you must, but smile if it kills you.' The notice makes an essentially serious point. It is that you can tolerate a lot of awkwardness in someone if they show by their face that they genuinely do not wish to be awkward without good cause. Put another way, if people show by their faces that they are doing their best to be pleasant to others, they will be allowed greater extremes of difficult and disruptive behaviour than those who are unpleasant in both action and manner.

The exercise for this chapter, then, is that you should attempt to practise the message in the notice. For the next week at least greet everyone you encounter in the course of your work with a pleasant smile, as if genuinely pleased to see them. You do not have to maintain an inane grin on your face. It is sufficient for this exercise that you at least meet people with a smile.

Note the reactions of others to your action. Do they return the smile? Does the encounter appear to proceed better or worse than it would normally do? Does anyone appear to be surprised? Or suspicious? Does the encounter last longer or is it shorter than it would otherwise be?

Of the people you meet several times during the week, does there appear to be any change taking place in the relationship between you? Is there any difference in the responses of men and those of women? Or in those of the young and those of the old? Or those of superiors, colleagues and subordinates? Or those of fellow workers in the organization and those of customers or clients?

Note your own reactions. Did you find the exercise easy or difficult? Did you feel at all silly in carrying it out? If so, why? Did you find your attitudes to people changing at all? Did you find yourself spending longer with people you dislike? Did you find yourself disliking them any less? How do you feel when others smile at you?

Try to keep a written or taped record of as many of the reactions as you can.

Exercise review

Let us now consider how the exercise has gone, if indeed it has gone at all typically. You will in all probability have noticed some at least of the following points:

1 Most people will have returned your greeting smile.

2 Most encounters will then have proceeded more smoothly than they would normally have done.

3 Some people, especially those with whom you have a relationship of mutual dislike, will have been surprised – but perhaps not unpleasantly – by your new approach. Some, however, will have reacted with suspicion and will have thought to themselves 'What's he [or she] up to?'

4 Encounters will probably have tended to last rather longer than they would otherwise have done. People tend to allow a pleasurable activity to be prolonged and will try to shorten an unpleasant one, for fairly obvious reasons.

5 You may well have found that, where you have met certain people several times during the week, your relationships with them have improved in some way.

6 Women tended to respond quicker and more favourably than men, if you are a man. If you are a woman, the reverse will probably be true.

7 Young people will have tended to respond more readily than older people.

8 Subordinates and colleagues will have generally responded better than superiors, though even here your more positive approach will not have gone unnoticed and may well pay off later.

9 Customers and clients will probably have responded much more readily than fellow workers. It is in such 'public contact' (as it is often called) that positive actions such as smiling are particularly important.

Now, how about your own reactions? Some points you may have noted are:

1 After some initial awkwardness, you should have found the exercise quite easy to carry out.

2 You should not have felt silly during the exercise. If you did, perhaps you were not following the instructions closely enough. Maybe you were inclined to grin or to keep the smile on your face a little too long.

3 You should have found your attitudes to others improving and becoming more positive.

4 You may well have found yourself spending more time with people you dislike and you might even have found yourself disliking them just a little less.

5 You must like it when others smile at you, surely? Well, remember that they will feel just as pleased when you smile at them.

The range of expressions

When you consider how many muscles there are in the human face, it is not surprising that the range of facial expressions we can produce is very wide. There are many subtleties in changes of expression which can be shown – consider, for instance, the great variety of smiles possible between the Mona Lisa's partial smile and an open grin. However, in communication, facial expressions are most commonly used to express a degree of emotion and there are a limited number of these most of us can in practice recognize with any reliability.

Two American researchers, Paul Eckman and Wallace Friesen, have discovered that there are six principal facial expressions which are used to show when people are happy, sad, disgusted, angry, afraid and interested (though the last is not really an emotion). They have found that these are about the only emotions most of us are likely to agree about when we see others expressing them. In this case, we might usefully look a little more closely at each of the six.

Smiles, though wide-ranging, can be categorized as: slight smiles, normal smiles (of the kind we hope you were using in the last exercise) and broad smiles. In a smile, the mouth is usually closed, but in open smiles the teeth can be showing. A broad smile with the teeth showing will usually be called a grin and grins can be classified as closed (with the teeth together) and open (with the teeth parted). Smiles are normally used as a greeting gesture and generally to indicate varying degrees of pleasure, amusement and happiness, though in some contexts they can show aggression, sarcasm and other negative feelings.

The converse emotional area, sadness, has no such single expression to typify it. Sadness, disappointment and depression are usually revealed by lack of expression and by such things as turning down of the corners of the mouth, a downward look and a general sagging of the features. Extremes of sadness will be characterized by the appearance of tears, trembling of the lips and attempts to shield the face from view.

Disgust and contempt are shown by a narrowing of the eyes and a grimacing mouth, which becomes more pronounced with increasing strength of the feeling. The nose will also probably be wrinkled up and the head turned aside to avoid having to look at the cause of the reaction.

Anger is most commonly characterized by steady gaze at the source of offence, frowning or scowling and a gritting of the teeth together. Some people go pale when angry, but others go red – and even a purplish colour – in extreme anger or fury. The whole body posture will be tense, as if ready to spring into immediate offensive action or attack.

Fear has no single expression to betray its presence. It may be shown in wide open eyes, an open mouth or by a general trembling which affects the face as much as the rest of the body. There may even be signs of perspiration and a paleness of colouring.

Interest is often indicated by what is called the 'head cock' – holding the head at an angle to the subject of interest. Interest may also be shown by eyes that are wider open than normal and a slightly open mouth (especially common in children who have their interest taken by something). When people are seated, the chin may be propped by the fingers if they are listening attentively.

These are just some of the many facial expressions to be watched for and noted in building up mastery of this aspect of body language (see Figure 2.1).

Figure 2.1 Can you correctly identify each of the emotions illustrated above? (a) Happiness, (b) Sadness, (c) Disgust/contempt, (d) Anger, (e) Fear, (f) Interest

Faces and first impressions

It is said that the most critical period in an encounter between two people is the first five minutes (one writer has even suggested it is as little as four minutes). The impressions formed in this time will tend to persist and even be reinforced by later behaviour, which will tend to be interpreted not objectively but in the light of these first impressions. We tend to note the occasions on which our first impressions of people were mistaken and had later to be revised because there are so few of them. Since the face is one of the first features we notice about a person it can clearly play a vital role in the process of establishing relationships with others.

A gesture which appears almost universally at the beginning of the greeting phase (especially when meeting people we know well) is the eyebrow flash. This consists of a rapid up and down movement of the eyebrows, with an accompanying smile, and it seems to show the person we are about to talk to that we are pleased to see them. In the case of people we know, it seems to operate as a gesture of recognition. It is widely used in both advanced and primitive societies.

When we first meet someone and look at their face, probably the first judgement we make is whether we like them or not; whether we find them attractive or unattractive. A good deal of evidence has been accumulated about what are generally regarded as attractive facial features. People shown photographs of a number of other people will usually agree on which are the handsome men and the beautiful women. Features that are commonly stated as contributing to attractiveness are well cut and styled hair, a high forehead, clear eyes, a smooth complexion, even teeth and a general symmetry of features (although research has shown that no-one's features are perfectly symmetrical).

But in these first few minutes we do more than simply decide whether or not we like someone. We make judgements about their character, personality, intelligence, temperament, personal habits, working abilities, suitability as a friend or lover, and so on. All of this is done on the basis of very little information about the other – and yet we are more often right in these judgements than we are wrong. Ask yourself how often you recall changing your first impression of someone and compare this with the total of all the people you have met. Alternatively, over the next week keep a record of all those you meet for the first time. In a couple of months' time review the record and decide in how many cases you had to change these first impressions. Chances are there won't be many (see also Chapter 13).

Talking with your face

Next to the eyes the face is the most powerful means by which we communicate non-verbally. We use it – and others rely on it for indications – to show how rewarding we are as individuals, to express our emotional state of the moment, to indicate how attentive we are to others, and so on. A smile tells people we are pleased to see them, a frown warns them off. A downcast look tells them we're not feeling too happy, a raised eyebrow and a twist to the mouth shows we are in playful mood. A head cocked on one side shows we are listening. We shut our eyes and the lecturer at the front of the class knows we have switched off.

We can say quite a lot with our faces. We can use facial expressions to communicate when words are inappropriate. Someone says something out of place and we try to show in our faces that they have committed a *faux pas*. In a noisy factory, words are totally useless but a friendly grin gets the message over.

Facial expressions can, however, be used to reinforce the impact of verbal messages. A mother scolds a child and her face tells her offspring that she really is displeased this time. A group of shop stewards tell the management their reaction to the latest pay offer and the set of their jaws tells the management to go away and come up with something better. At an official gathering, two totally opposed individuals make polite conversation, but their frosty faces betray their mutual animosity.

It is clear from what has been said so far that the face's main role in our use of body language lies in the expression of emotions. As we saw earlier, there is a limited number of emotions that can be reliably recognized by observers of the face. Nevertheless, the face undoubtedly has a contribution to make, not only to the expression of any emotion but also to the expression of any degree of emotion – no matter how subtle. This is a point which will apply to the degree that many other parts of the body contribute to our use of body language, and we should not mislead ourselves into thinking that many messages are simply and clearly conveyed by one part of the body alone. Most messages are context-dependent when it comes to fully understanding them.

Another aspect which deserves consideration is how far artefacts contribute to non-verbal messages. Such artefacts can include moustaches, beards, spectacles, ear-rings and the use of make-up. Since such things change our appearance we need to take into account their effects upon how others will perceive us. For instance, moustaches will often be taken to indicate greater age than a clean-shaven upper lip, which may be a reason for their popularity with young men. Beards may be taken as a sign of an independent mind which resists pressures to conform. Spectacles often lead to individuals being credited with greater intelligence than they actually possess. Ear-rings, if worn by men, may be interpreted as a sign of effeminacy, though some boys currently wear them as a defiant gesture of emerging masculinity. A girl who wears heavy make-up risks (often unfounded) conclusions concerning her moral standards.

From this we can see that we do not always send the non-verbal messages we intend to send. The more we are aware of such pitfalls in the unspoken language of the body, the better we shall be able to use it.

Face facts

Research into facial expressions has not only explored their role in expressing emotions, then; it has also examined their role in revealing personality, attitudes towards others, sexual attraction and attractiveness, the desire to communicate or initiate interaction, and the degree of expressiveness when communicating. It has also produced some other rather interesting findings.

Facial expressions can be affected by a person's state of health. It has been found that before a woman undergoes childbirth her face shows more signs of anxiety and stress, though those who have had a child already usually show fewer signs. People who have ulcers frown more than those who haven't. Depressed patients have been found to smile more widely after having electro-convulsive therapy than before it.

Different parts of the face are attended to when observers are perceiving different emotions. Fear is usually looked for in the eyes, as is sadness. Happiness is seen in the cheeks and the mouth as well as in the eyes. Surprise is seen in the forehead, eyes and mouth movements. Anger is perceived from the appearance of the whole face and not just from the brows and the colour of the face as many people suppose.

The expression on the face, when people are communicating, is constantly changing. Amongst the changes new research techniques have enabled us to identify are micromomentary facial expressions. These last for a fraction of a second, as their name implies, and often indicate a person's true feelings. For example, a person may be saying that he is pleased to see someone and may be smiling but may reveal his true attitude with a micromomentary expression of disgust. Such expressions are too fleeting for most people to perceive them, but they can be captured by the camera. Research like this offers many possibilities of using body language to discover what others are really thinking and feeling.

A number of studies have been made of individuals' abilities to copy the facial expressions of others. Most were able to copy better with the aid of a mirror but very anxious individuals tended to do better without a mirror. Apparently, no one has yet followed up this research by investigating the practical applications, for example, in counselling work. Some studies have also suggested that when individuals copied smiles they felt happier, which has some interesting possibilities that we shall be studying in the next section of this chapter.

Differences have been observed in the ways men and women use facial expressions when communicating. Women tend to laugh and smile more than men, but more often because they find the situation slightly uncomfortable than out of greater sociability.

People tend to talk less, make more speech errors and smile more when attempting to deceive others than when being completely open and honest. Nurses' ability to deceive by the expression on their faces correlated with their subsequent effectiveness in their work, as judged by superiors. Since nurses often have to conceal from ill patients just how ill they are, this finding is perhaps not surprising but it does suggest that people, like nurses, who spend their working lives dealing with other people should receive training in the use of body language.

One psychologist has found that people judge things such as criminality from the face. A number of photographs of innocent people were shown and subjects were asked to allocate such crimes as armed robbery and rape to the appropriate faces. A significant number of people, for instance, picked out one unfortunate innocent as a rapist. Research like this tends to make one uneasy, not only about, say, police identification parades but also about the signals we may unwittingly be sending to others about our own attitudes, personality and behaviour.

Smile, you'll feel better

Because the smile is probably the most universally used and the most positive facial expression, it will be useful if we examine it in a little more detail here. Smiles are used all over the world to indicate or reflect pleasure or happiness. Even children who have been blind from birth smile when they are pleased. Smiles are also used to show reassurance, amusement and even ridicule. We shall be concerned here with the positive uses to which smiles can be put.

Smiles are rarely used deliberately, but they can be. Experiments have shown that if individuals are asked to smile and are then shown pictures of various events, they report that the pictures please them and even make them feel elated. If individuals are asked to frown during the same kind of experiment, they report experiencing feelings of annoyance and even anger. Research like this perhaps provides some scientific support for the popular saying 'Laugh and the world laughs with you'.

Smiles can also be used to mask other emotions. An athlete who loses to a particularly disliked opponent will still try to smile bravely to hide his disappointment. A smile may also be a submissive response to ward off another's attack. Those who work in occupations that bring them into contact with the public, such as receptionists or aircraft cabin crew, are trained to use smiles to reassure clients and passengers. Smiling may be used to make a tense situation more comfortable. A smile will tend to call forth a smile from the other person and thus ease away the tension.

The best time to test the power of the smile is when you least feel like smiling, whether through illness or depression. Force a smile on to your face and keep it there for as long as possible. Each time the smile disappears, wait a few minutes and then try again. Within a short time, you should notice a distinct improvement in how you feel. This technique will not always work, but very often it will and is certainly at least worth a try. Of all the facial expressions that we use, the smile is the one most worth encouraging in ourselves.

EXERCISES AND EXPERIMENTS

1 Good morning, world!

There are two versions of this experiment – one for the timid and one for the bold. The timid should select people they know, the bold can try it on anyone they meet. When you go out tomorrow morning, do not smile when greeting people you meet in the street. Count how many smile. The following morning smile warmly in greeting at everyone you meet. Count how many return your smile. What's the difference? The bold will find the greatest difference. It's surprising how many strangers will smile if you smile first. It's as if they want to all the time but are just a little afraid to take the initiative.

2 Face exercises

To develop muscle tone (get rid of flabbiness and a sagging face), try each of these exercises for one minute every day:

   a Starting from the face at rest, grin broadly, preferably lifting the eyebrows at the same time.

   b Starting from the face at rest, pucker the lips into a tight round 'O'.

   c Starting from the face at rest, lift the chin as high as it will go, raise your eyebrows and alternately grin and pucker.

Do these exercises in front of a mirror if you can.

3 Stop frowning

Whenever you have any concentrating to do, place your palm across your forehead. If you find you are frowning, stop it. If you have to move your face at all, try raising your eyebrows so that your forehead creases horizontally rather than vertically. You will find that one result of this exercise is to make you less prone to headaches.

4 Show your feelings

In front of a mirror, practise each of the following emotions in sequence:

   a happiness
   b sadness
   c surprise
   d disgust
   e fear
   f anger.

If you can secure the cooperation of someone else, see if they can identify each emotion from your expression. Vary the sequence to make the task a little more difficult for them. This exercise will tell you how well you express your feelings. It will also tell you how good your partner is at recognizing emotions. You can reverse roles once your partner has fully grasped the nature of the exercise and you may even be able to involve others. It can make a useful little party game, with points given for accuracy in recognition.

5 Is your face your fortune?

Collect six photographs of people's faces, one of which should be a well known attractive film or TV star. Show them to as large a number of people as possible and ask them to rate the attractiveness of each face on a scale of 1 to 10. Do you find others' ratings agree with your own? Do they tend to agree on the most attractive face amongst the six? The exercise should provide some fascinating insights into people's perceptions of others.

6 How many faces?

Study the faces of those you meet. Can they be classified into types? Do similar ones keep cropping up? Or is every one unique?

3 | HEAD MOVEMENTS

If you watch two people talking, you will notice that, in addition to the movement of their mouths and changes in facial expression as they talk, their heads move in what may appear to be quite random ways. Not so. These movements are no more random than the eye movements and facial expressions we have already examined. In this chapter we shall consider some of the ways in which we can use our heads to help us speak body language more effectively.

The most obvious and perhaps most frequently used head movement is the nod. Over most of the world it signifies agreement, affirmation or approval and can therefore be very useful when verbal language differences make communication difficult. We shall make a particular study of this.

Head movements are important not only in talking but also in listening for, as we shall see, if they are used properly they can help us to communicate more easily and if they are misused they can quickly affect adversely a relationship with another person. A nod must not be used when a shake would be more appropriate, and vice versa. There are times when the head should be bowed and times it should be held erect.

Head movements can be used as speech markers, in social acknowledgements, as gestural 'echoes' (we shall look at this phenomenon in more detail in the next chapter), and to indicate our attitude towards an encounter and how we see our role within it. They are, then, capable of much greater versatility and subtlety in expression than might be supposed and there are many individual movements whose significance and usefulness to us we shall explore. We shall find that there are many more ways in which we can use our heads than we ever thought possible.

We will need to remember not to try to interpret head movements in isolation. The focus of our attention in this chapter is on how the head moves – but this does not mean forgetting all about the effects other elements of body language can have. A good example is the wink. This may seem to be simply an eye movement, but it is also a facial expression and, since the head usually moves slightly to one side when winking, it is a head movement. Only when one is winking surreptitiously will there be no head movement. In fact, the presence or absence of head movement can be a crucial factor in interpreting the significance of a wink.

EXERCISE: ON THE NOD

Because the head nod is such a common movement, it will be useful for us to base the main chapter exercise on it. Select a conversation with someone you know well. As they talk, nod your head encouragingly. Do they seem to do more of the talking or less?

On another occasion, with the same person, as they talk do not nod your head at all. Do they seem to do more of the talking or less?

After each conversation, record your impressions in your notebook or on tape.

Repeat the exercise with a stranger and record your impressions in the same way.

Now, preferably with the same people, nod for half the conversation and then stop. What happens?

Note down your own feelings about the exercise. Did you find it easy or difficult to do? Which parts were the easiest and which the most difficult?

Consider how other people use nods when they are talking to you. Observe interviewers on television, preferably with the sound turned off. What kinds of things do you notice about nodding behaviour? Do people nod most when talking or listening? Why do you think this is? Are there any other things you notice about the ways people use nods in face-to-face communication?

Exercise review

Now let us look at what you might have discovered. The comments offered here will also be relevant when we return to the subject of head nods later in this chapter.

In the first part of the exercise, nodding your head should have encouraged the other person to speak more and for longer. Refusing to nod should have resulted in the other person drying up and ending the conversation very quickly. You should have had the same experiences when conversing with a stranger, except that you may have noticed that the stranger stopped talking quicker when head nods are absent than someone you know well.

When you were nodding for half the conversation and not for the other half, you should have seen similar responses. The first half of the conversation will almost certainly have gone much better than the second half. The other person will have conversed much more freely and easily when you were nodding than when you were not.

As far as your own feelings are concerned, you will almost certainly have felt more comfortable and at ease when you were allowed to nod. In fact, you may even have found it impossible not to nod at times.

In observing other people's nodding behaviour, you should have noticed that most people nod much more when they are listening than when they are talking. Television interviewers, for instance, nod when they are listening to interviewees' answers precisely because it encourages them to open up and talk more fully about the subject. Nodding, as we shall see later, is a major way of showing that we are attending to what another person is saying.

Talking heads

As with other aspects of body language, head movements can be used for a variety of purposes. They can be used to indicate attitudes, to replace speech and to support what is said. They can even contradict what is said and if this happens, as in other forms of body talk, what the head movements say will be believed in preference to the words uttered.

Let us, for example, take the role of head movements in expressing, whether consciously or unconsciously, a person's attitudes. When the head is held high and possibly tilted slightly backward, this is often interpreted as being prompted by a haughty and even aggressive attitude (if accompanied by such things as a fixed stare, a curl to the lips and an unusually red – or occasionally white – face). A lowered head indicates submissiveness or humility or even depression (if accompanied by such factors as slow and infrequent low-voiced speech, a general sagging in posture and an avoidance of eye contact).

Head movements have an interesting use as speech markers. Slight head nods, sweeps to one side and chin thrusts act as stresses, when speaking, to place emphasis on certain words and phrases. The kind of context in which this type of behaviour is most readily observed is the public speech, where it is necessary to have rather more dramatic emphasis than in everyday conversation. This applies to gestures, too.

The head can be used to point in those situations in which finger pointing would be considered inappropriate or even rude. The head is moved to indicate the direction in which one wants someone to look or move. It is also often used by the chairs of meetings to indicate who is the next person to have his or her permission to speak.

It is interesting to watch people's heads as they are speaking (television without the sound is a good medium to use) in order to observe the small but rhythmic movements made by the head in accompaniment to speech. If you do this, see if you can, for instance, match the head movement to the end of a sentence. It is normally marked by a slight downward movement, with a slight pause before the head moves again.

Listening heads

We have already encountered the use of the head nod in listening behaviour (in the exercise at the beginning of this chapter) and, because it is of such key importance to our mastery of body language, we shall return to it at the end. But there are other behaviours that are important to efficient listening.

One of these is the direction in which the head is pointing. It is always difficult to accept that someone is listening to us if they are looking away from us. If they are indeed listening, we expect that they will at least be looking at us. Why this should be so is not clear because it is obviously quite possible to be listening intently even if your eyes are closed and you are facing in the opposite direction. Nevertheless, listening, like many other things, it appears, must not only be done but must be seen to be done.

Another behaviour is the 'head cock', holding the head at a tilted angle to the person being listened to (Figure 3.1). It is used very much by animals, especially dogs, and also by children, who even use it when speaking to another person whose attention they are seeking to secure – almost as if they were showing the other person how he or she ought to be behaving if they were to exhibit the desired degree of attention.

Figure 3.1 Two versions of the head cock

When we are listening to others we tend unconsciously to copy their head movements. It is almost as if we wish to demonstrate a commonality of interest by a commonality of behaviour.

It is also quite common, when listening in a reasonably intimate setting, to bring the head closer to the person being listened to. The *tête-à-tête* (or head-to-head talk) can even become literally true in the case of lovers whispering quietly to each other. Physical closeness is used as an indication of intellectual and emotional closeness.

When listening in a seated position, the head is often propped by the thumb and the first two fingers of the hand. This is widely interpreted by speakers as a sign of intelligent interest. Care must be taken, however, for if the chin is propped in the palm (and especially if the eyelids begin to droop) it may be taken as an indication of boredom, with both the speaker and what he or she is saying.

Efficient listening, then, is by no means purely passive. An active use of the kind of behaviour outlined above can help to show speakers that they are receiving your full and undivided attention – or that they are not.

It depends on how you look at it

The orientation of your head when looking at people can have a marked effect upon their interpretation of your behaviour. One of the reasons that makes it possible for you to look at someone 'out of the corner of your eye' is that, as indicated above, people will expect the focus of your attention to be where you are looking. This is not infallible, however, and if the direction of gaze is too obviously at variance with the direction of the head or if sideways glances are too long or too frequent they will be spotted.

Although indirect observation is frequently not a socially acceptable activity, using head movements to indicate a lack of seriousness in one's attitudes may well be. Tilting the head to one side (in a similar manner to the head cock described above) can be used to indicate that what one is saying is not intended to be taken seriously. It can also be used as an appealing gesture, particularly by young attractive girls when talking to young men in a flirtatious or playful manner. It may be used in greetings, accompanied by the 'eyebrow flash' discussed in Chapter 2, in order to achieve an extra degree of friendliness in the greeting.

The head can be used aggressively. Thrust forward from the shoulders, it poses a threat to an opponent and, in the often horrifying tactic of the teenage hooligan in the form of a headbutt, it can even be used as a weapon. Less aggressive people, like politicians making forceful speeches, can use the head in small sharp downwards movements to add emphasis to particular words and phrases.

There are sex differences in the use of head movements, as in many other aspects of the use of body language. Women use the head cock more than men and are often shown in advertisements and magazine pictures with tilted heads. Men tilt their heads forward in a greeting nod more than women. Women are more frequently observed with the head lowered in a submissive gesture than are men. It may be that such differences in behaviour are non-verbal markers in social interaction of differences in gender. It may also be that, as women become increasingly liberated, such differences between the sexes will become less marked.

How to use your head

As we have seen, you can use your head for many more things than just keeping your ears apart. In this section we will review what we have learned about head movements and highlight those that we can make practical use of in the future.

First of all, head movements are useful as a means of social acknowledgement. Men tend to use a nod to signify that they have seen and recognized someone; women tend to use a head tilt. There is no reason why these behaviours should continue unchanged in the future, but it may be more effective socially to follow the convention of the company in which you find yourself.

Head movements can be used to beckon someone in circumstances where a shout or even a wave would be inappropriate. This beckoning movement takes the form of a diagonal throwing back of the head and may be repeated several times, depending on the urgency of the 'come here' request.

To express doubt or reluctance, the head is sometimes swayed or rocked from side to side, as if weighing a request or a proposition in the balance. To express disdain or haughtiness, it may be tossed or shaken, in much the same way that a defiant horse tosses its head. This gesture is probably more frequently used by women than men. A gesture more commonly used by men is the head swivel, which takes the form of turning the head to look at the object or person newly observed. It often occurs when a man catches sight of, or has his attention drawn to the presence of, an attractive woman.

Winking, accompanied by a short, sharp downward tilt of the head to one side, is a useful gesture. It can show that a statement is not meant to be taken seriously. It can be humorously conspiratorial, saying 'You and I are in this together', or, 'This is a secret between the two of us'. It can simply be used as a gesture of friendly social acknowledgement.

Head movements can express attitudes and it may be better, therefore, unless you want to appear humble or submissive, to hold your head reasonably erect. This will also tend to encourage good posture.

Nod if you want me to continue

The head nod signifies agreement, approval, acceptance, continuing attention and understanding according to the context in which it is used. Broadly speaking, the strength of the nod (that is, the degree of up and down movement) declines through these categories.

The largest nods usually indicate agreement, whilst the slightest nods can provide a speaker with feedback on how well he is being understood. As with other body movements, however, the further away the speaker is, the greater the degree of movement has to be in order to be accurately perceived.

The least obvious, and yet in many ways the most effective, use of the head nod is in showing continued attention. As you probably found in the exercises at the beginning of this chapter, nodding fairly frequently (but not continuously) when someone is speaking encourages them to speak for longer and to say more. A number of research studies have quantified this and have shown that the amount of speech that can be generated in this way can be three or four times greater than normal. It is a finding which is of important practical value to the process of making interviews and discussions more productive and effective. Refusal by a listener to nod can cause a speaker to dry up completely without knowing why, apart from experiencing a vague feeling that the listener was not really attending even if he or she was looking at the speaker most of the time.

Training courses in the use of body language should make a particular point of showing these various uses of the head nod. It is a technique which has an importance quite out of proportion to its apparent significance. In this it is comparable to the techniques of using eye contact discussed in Chapter 1 and is commonly used by a listener in combination with an increased amount of eye contact.

Nodding is also important, as we have seen, in enabling a speaker, especially a public speaker, to emphasize particular words and phrases. Here, it needs to be used with some degree of discrimination. Otherwise it can, like any other technique of giving emphasis to statements, lose much of its effect. Too much repetition removes the impact of any emphasizing technique.

As men tend to use head nods more than women, it may well be useful for women to practise using head nods rather more. However, there is some evidence to suggest that women are thought to be better listeners than men and this may mean that it is only when speaking that women need to use more head nods.

EXERCISES AND EXPERIMENTS

1 Head cock

Look for instances where other people use head cocks. Watch young children who have not yet learned to speak fluently, if you can. They seem to make more use of body language, almost certainly because of their lack of verbal skill. In your encounters with others try using head cocks a little more to show interest. Don't make them too obvious or exaggerated or the result will simply look silly. You should find people begin to speak to you more.

2 *Tête-à-tête*

Look for examples of people talking with their heads touching or very close together. Is it only lovers who converse in this way? You should find that those who want to prevent others overhearing them keep their heads closer together – for example, businessmen, or a group telling dirty stories (note how the latter move apart when laughing at the punch line).

3 Head dance

Watch a TV discussion programme without the sound and concentrate on the participants' head movements. Note how the slight movements up, to the left, to the right, and down seem to have a pattern to them. Note also how the end of a sentence seems to be matched not only with a pause but also with a downward movement of the head.

4 What can your head say?

Using the information given in this chapter and any other sources you can find, make a list of all the messages that head movements alone can convey to others. But remember, it must be the head alone.

4 | GESTURES AND BODY MOVEMENTS

It is in the use of gestures that our mastery of body language can achieve real eloquence. Eye contact, facial expression and head movements, though of vital importance, have certain limitations. Gestures permit a degree of expressiveness and subtlety that is not possible with other aspects of non-verbal communication. It is the use of gestures to convey meaning that most people think of when they talk about body language and in this chapter we shall consider the variety of messages for which gestures can be the vehicles.

Several writers have attempted to classify gestures into categories. Michael Argyle has suggested that there are five different functions that gestures can serve:

- illustrations and other speech-linked signals
- conventional signs and sign languages
- movements which express emotions
- movements which express personality
- movements which are used in various religious and other rituals.

Paul Eckman and Wallace Friesen have also suggested that there are five groupings, but their categories are:

- emblems (movements that are substitutes for words)
- illustrators (movements that accompany speech)
- regulators (movements that maintain or signal a change in a person's listening or speaking role)
- adaptors (movements such as scratching one's head, rubbing one's hands or fiddling with objects which tend to cast light upon a person's emotional state)
- affect displays (movements which more directly reveal emotions, as facial expressions do).

However they are classified, gestures can be used to express a range of attitudes, emotions and other messages. Michael Argyle quotes a number of conventional gestures which seem to have almost universal meanings. Examples are shaking the fist to show anger, rubbing the palms together in anticipation, clapping as a sign of approval, raising one's hand to gain attention, yawning out of boredom, patting someone on the back to encourage them, and rubbing the stomach to indicate hunger. Gerard Nierenberg and Henry Calero suggest that gestures are used in expressing, amongst many other things, openness, defensiveness, readiness, reassurance, frustration, confidence, nervousness, acceptance, expectancy, relationships and suspicion. They show that these gestures are used even in situations in which the other person cannot be seen, as when making a telephone call or using a tape recorder.

It is this richness of silent communication that we shall now begin to explore. But first, as in other chapters, let us attempt an exercise which will put us in the right frame of mind for what is to come.

EXERCISE: EVERYDAY MIME

Find a situation that you can observe where people cannot communicate with each other by using words, because it is too noisy, because silence is necessary, because they are too far apart to hear each other, or there is some other barrier to spoken communication. Examples might include a noisy factory, a TV studio, a restaurant, a building site, a hospital, a library or an examination hall. Look for, and note down, gestures used in such contexts to attract attention, to direct, to tell someone there is a telephone call for them, to beckon, to greet and bid goodbye, to indicate passage of time, to keep quiet, and to convey any other messages that gestures can be used for.

What similarities and differences do you notice? What examples of special codes do you come across? How successful do gestures seem to be as a means of communication? What are their advantages? What are their limitations?

How useful are gestures when communicating with someone who does not speak your language? What kinds of needs or requests can most easily be conveyed by gestures? Which are the most difficult to express? Which are impossible to express? How well do words translate into gestures? How well can gestures express emotions? How well can they express or request detailed information?

As a further alternative, if you can secure the cooperation of a group of people (for instance, if you are a member of a class which is using this book), you can play charades or a version of the game in which two teams try to guess the title of a film, TV show, radio programme or book and get points for succeeding within a time limit of, say, two minutes. This can be not only a good exercise in using gestures but also great fun – there is, after all, no reason at all why learning should not be enjoyable.

What kinds of situations or titles are easiest to guess from gestures alone? What kinds of people are best at communicating through gestures? Why do some people seem to be incapable of getting a message over through gestures? What are the secrets of successful charades playing? How do you identify the key elements in situations or titles for communication through gestures and body movements?

Exercise review

Where you noticed similar gestures being used in widely different contexts, you have probably witnessed 'universal' gestures or conventional gestures of the kind referred to earlier. You should have noticed that gestures become more deliberate and even exaggerated with increasing distance between those involved. You might have noticed a difference in the gestures used indoors and those used outdoors, with indoor gestures being more controlled and subtle. You may have noticed differences between men and women, adults and children (a fascinating area for gesture study is of very young children at playgroups) or people in different social classes in the gestures they use; that the gestures used during daytime differ from those used at night, as do gestures used at work and those used in leisure contexts.

You will probably have found that people at work seem to have their own codes for the meanings of gestures. This is especially noticeable in places like TV studios, where silence on the part of non-participant studio floor staff is essential. You may have concluded that gestures are useful but that their usefulness has certain limitations. The advantages of gestures are that they assist communication where people cannot speak to each other easily, they can act as a kind of convenient shorthand and they can add an interesting degree of expressiveness to everyday social interaction. Their restrictions are that the amount of information they can convey is limited, certain things cannot be communicated by gesture alone (try explaining your name and address by gestures alone), and in certain contexts they can simply be unsuitable (for example, to warn someone of impending danger). If you have been able to observe people of different languages trying to converse, you will almost certainly have noticed that they rely heavily on gestures.

Simple, basic needs with which everyone is familiar (like hunger and thirst) are easier to communicate than complex or sophisticated ones (such as the location of the best night club or a particular brand of product which is not on display). Some messages may be so long and involved as to defy communication by gesture at all. Generally speaking, nouns and verbs translate more easily into gestures than adjectives, adverbs and other words. Gestures are probably most useful in expressing attitudes and emotions, which is true for most other aspects of body language.

If you played charades or the title-guessing game, you probably found that situations or titles which contain reference to action or movement were easier to communicate by gesture than those referring to abstract qualities (like truth, justice, democracy and belief) or to stationary objects (like house, road, fence and chair – you usually need to gesture the shape of things like this, which is cheating a little). You probably found that outgoing and sociable people are better at this kind of game than the shy and retiring, though often the latter have hidden talents which only need bringing out. Some people are so self-conscious they cannot communicate in this way at all. This book should help such people to relax, even if they don't actually do any of the exercises. The secrets of successful charades playing and portrayal of titles are to concentrate on actions and movement, then on shapes, then on those elements similar to other activities that can be easily conveyed by gestures (such as getting the 'Tale' across by gesturing a wagging tail in *Tale of Two Cities* – 'City' is an example of a very difficult word to convey, but most people will guess it if they get the first three words).

Let your body do the talking

Any part of the body can be used to make a gesture. We have already considered the use of the head (see Chapter 3). If here we work our way down the rest of the body, we shall be able to identify most of the other gestures and body movements that have communicative value.

This aspect of body language is usually called *kinesics*. This is a term coined by an American researcher, Ray Birdwhistell, who was one of the first to study body–motion communication when serious interest in it began in the late 1940s. A *kine* is the smallest observable unit of body movement and kinesics refers to the scientific study of gestures and other body movements.

The most common shoulder movement is the shrug, which usually conveys the messages 'I don't know', 'I don't care', 'I am doubtful', or 'What can you do?' (i.e. this situation is really hopeless). It is an up and down movement of both shoulders and may be accompanied by appropriate facial expressions and head movements. A single shoulder being shrugged usually means, 'Take your hand off my arm (or shoulder)' or 'Leave me alone'.

The chest can be puffed out as a gesture of pride or achievement but it is commonly only used in a humorous and self-mocking way. Someone who used it seriously would probably be considered conceited.

The stomach can be sucked in as if to say, 'I am really fit' or 'I'm not as fat as I look'. Even though men do tend unconsciously to hold their stomachs in when in the presence of an attractive girl, this gesture is also used only half-seriously.

The pelvis and the buttocks can be used to make gestures, but most of them are interpreted by others as sexual invitations and are often considered obscene. Perhaps if you need to use such gestures as invitations it is a sign that your mastery of body language is, to say the least, unsophisticated.

The arms, hands and fingers are used for a great variety of gestures, and we will look at some of these in a little more detail in the next section. We shall be selective for it would simply not be practicable to consider all the possibilities. One interesting hand gesture, however, is *steepling*. In this the tips of the fingers are placed together in what resembles an attitude of prayer except that the palms are kept well apart. Nierenberg and Calero quote this as a gesture which signifies confidence, or at least a desire to make a listener think one feels confident.

Legs can be crossed or uncrossed and many writers have tried to put all kinds of messages into these gestures. It may be an exaggeration to suggest that when a woman crosses her legs and pulls her skirt down to cover her knees she is cutting off the possibility of an approach, but it is interesting that women will usually sit with their legs crossed even when they customarily wear jeans or trousers. Men seem to be quite happy on occasion to lounge around in an open-legged posture.

Feet can be interesting. When they tap or twitch they can be examples of *leakage*, that is, a person is trying to conceal some attitude or information from others and is not quite succeeding. Someone who plays poker regularly may always know when one of his friends has a good hand because, despite having the traditional give-nothing-away poker-face, his foot twitches. Such leakage usually occurs in the lower half of the body, probably because we take more trouble to control things like facial expressions.

Another interesting phenomenon is the *gestural echo*. Watch a group of people conversing and note how, when one person uses a gesture, others will use it later. As we shall see in the next chapter, something similar happens with posture. It also happens, incidentally, with words during conversations.

Morris's gesture maps

Desmond Morris was a very popular writer on the subject of non-verbal communication. He and a team of researchers from Oxford University published a guide to the origins and distribution of twenty selected gestures. From information gathered from forty

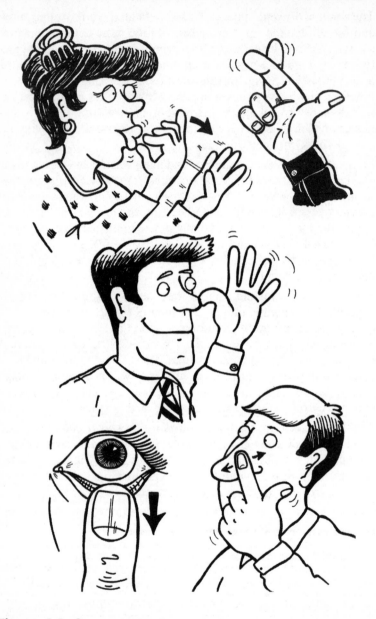

Figure 4.1   Some common gestures

places across Europe, they were able to identify how commonly each of the gestures occurred and what meanings were attached to them. Their findings indicate how important it often is to know the context in which a gesture is used before trying to interpret its meaning. They also show that a gesture in one part of Europe can sometimes have the opposite meaning from its usual meaning in another. Some of these are illustrated in Figure 4.1.

The first gesture Morris's team studied was the *Fingertip Kiss*. In this, the tips of the fingers and thumb are kissed and then the hand is moved quickly away from the mouth and the fingers spread out. It is symbolic of the mouth kiss, which is a gesture used all over the world to show affection. The gesture is most commonly used to indicate praise in Spain, France, Germany and Greece. In Portugal, Sardinia and Sicily it is used as a greeting. Its use is relatively rare in the British Isles and in Italy.

A gesture which appeared to have a common meaning all over Europe was the *Nose Thumb*, in which the thumb is placed on the end of the nose and the fingers are fanned out and sometimes waggled. It is generally used as a gesture of mockery or insult.

The *Fingers Cross*, in which the first and middle fingers are twisted around each other and the remaining fingers are held under the thumb, in contrast, has several meanings. Its main purpose is as a gesture of protection. When someone tells a lie they will cross their fingers (sometimes using both hands) in the superstitious belief that this will prevent the wrath of the gods falling on them for their deceit. This meaning is most common in the British Isles and Scandinavia. In Turkey, the gesture is used to break a friendship. Elsewhere it is used to indicate that something is good or OK, to swear an oath, or as a symbol for copulation.

The *Eyelid Pull*, in which the forefinger is placed on the cheekbone and pulled down to open the eye a little wider, means 'I am alert' in France, Germany, Yugoslavia and Turkey. In Spain and Italy, it means 'Be alert'. In Austria, it was found to signal boredom.

The *Nose Tap*, in which the forefinger is tapped on the side of the nose, conveys complicity, confidentiality or an instruction to main-tain secrecy in the British Isles and Sardinia. In Italy, it means 'Be alert'. If the tap is to the front of the nose, it can mean 'Mind your own business' in the British Isles, Holland and Austria.

The gesture maps that Desmond Morris and his team constructed for their twenty selected gestures were, to say the least, fascinating. But they can have a practical value as well. For instance, one gesture, The *Thumb Up*, is widely used to request lifts by hitch-hikers the world over. If they are travelling through parts of Belgium, Sicily, Sardinia, Malta or Greece, however, they should be aware that it may be interpreted as a sexual insult.

Peoplewatching

Many other people have carried out observations and research into gestures since at least 1600, and the study of gesture can be said to date back to Ancient Rome, with Cicero's *De Oratore*. People have been watching other people and recording and interpreting their gestures for a very long time indeed.

Recent research has been more scientific and systematic. Much of it has focused on what happens when body language is not used normally. Psychiatric patients, as one of their symptoms, exhibit variations of non-verbal behaviour which, by the very fact of being unusual, reflect a useful light on what is customary in everyday social interaction. From such clinical studies the late Albert Scheflen, a distinguished American psychiatrist, identified what he called *quasi-courtship behaviours*. These are behaviours which are normal in the courtship by one person of another, but which mentally ill patients often use inappropriately towards their therapists or other patients; they can, however, also be observed in everyday life when one person is attracted to another. Courtship readiness is usually signalled by such things as high muscle tone, reduced eye-bagginess and jowl sag, decreased slouch, and less stomach and shoulder sag. Preening behaviours can be observed – these include stroking one's hair, straightening one's tie or other clothing, and re-applying make-up. There are also actions of appeal or invitation such as flirtatious glances, leg-crossing to expose a thigh, and so on.

Other research has identified a phenomenon known as *gestural synchrony*. As a person speaks, his or her bodily movements keep pace in a kind of dance with the rhythms of speech. Listeners' movements also dance to the same 'tune', as it were, as the speaker's. In mentally ill patients, this rhythm is missing – another illustration of how we only notice the existence of something when it is not there: conspicuous by its absence, in fact.

Ekman and Friesen noted that certain gestures accompany certain attitudes. A rotating shrug of the hands accompanies feelings of uncertainty and confusion. A hand toss goes with the expression of feeling unable to control one's behaviour. Repetitious foot sliding is noticeable when patients are admitted to psychiatric institutions whereas, on leaving, foot gestures are generally more varied and active.

One research team found that where people are active, with many non-verbal movements, they will be rated as warm, more casual, agreeable and energetic. When the same people are still, with few movements, they will be considered more logical, cold and analytic. It is interesting to note the equation of movement with energy. Clearly, if you want to give an impression of drive and enthusiasm, say, in an interview, you can do it by increased use of gestures.

Some interesting studies have been made of regularities in the act of taking leave of someone. In the last minute or so of an encounter, the person seeking to end it breaks eye contact, leans forward and nods frequently. The peak of such activity occurs in the last fifteen seconds before standing. If one is not then released from the encounter a degree of frustration is experienced because it means the whole procedure has to be gone through again. A clearer example of the importance of attending to others' signals would be difficult to find.

Gesture psychology

The kinds of gestures that individuals use can be related to, and can vary with, other psychological factors. For instance, personality has a marked effect upon the numbers and varieties of gestures used. Also, we use gestures to enable us to make an assessment about the kind of personality an individual has.

One piece of research has reported that a majority of women who sit with their knees and feet together with legs extended have a personality associated with a desire for neatness and orderliness in work, a liking for making plans, a dislike of change and uncertainty, and a preference for organizing life according to a rigid schedule. Another has shown that authoritarian personalities tend to use less bodily movement than anti-authoritarians. Daughters without fathers have been found to use more self-touching gestures than those with fathers. Daughters of divorcees show more forward lean, more arm and leg openness, and make more than three times as many gesticulations or expressive hand movements as girls who lost their fathers before the age of five.

One researcher has found that when individuals are listening to a physically handicapped speaker they make fewer and smaller gestures than normal. This may be caused by some uncertainty about how to interact with a disabled person.

As far as sex differences in gesture behaviour are concerned, it has been found that men make more seating position shifts than women. If put through two interviews, men in the second interview make smaller gestures and move their feet less. For women, the reverse is true. The reason may be that men feel more at ease in the second interview whereas women find a second one more stressful than the first.

Some research has shown that, where two people in conversation use the same kind of gestures and body movements, they will perceive themselves as being similar and will like each other better. From this kind of study it may also be concluded that, where people are trying to communicate, similarities in gestural styles may be helpful. Such similarities can provide a background of rapport which may not even be consciously noticed.

Open and positive gestures and body movements are more influential when seeking to persuade someone to your point of view. Openness and confidence in movement are consistently rated by participants in experiments as being more active, positive and potent than closed or hesitant gestures and body movements (see Exercise 4 on page 56).

How to speak body language

From what has been said so far in this chapter about the various ways in which gestures are used in self-expression, it will be clear that there are ways of using gestures and body movements to greater effect.

When using any particular gesture, you should consider the context carefully to be sure the gesture is appropriate for it. Bear in mind that people from different parts of the world may understand a gesture to mean something very different from what you intend. Avoid gestures which are open to misinterpretation. Women crossing their legs, and revealing an expanse of thigh in the process, can often convey meanings they certainly do not intend. Gestures, especially of the lower part of the body, may provide an observer with leakage of true feelings you may prefer to conceal.

A useful gesture when attempting to convey a degree of confidence or assurance is steepling, provided it is not done too obviously or artificially. Gestural echoes can be a useful way of indicating a general sense of identity or sympathy with a group, provided it does not become too obvious an attempt at mimicry.

You should try to be as observant as possible of other people's gestures: like all forms of body language they can provide a very informative accompaniment to what is actually said. Much about a person's personality and attitudes can be inferred from how active they are in gesturing.

Quasi-courtship gestures can be useful in telling you what your relationship is with a member of the opposite sex. Watch for signs of a lack of synchrony between speech rhythms and body rhythms as this may offer clues to a person's emotional stability and general mental health. Be sensitive to others' gestures when it appears the end of an encounter is approaching. There is usually little purpose to be served by refusing to release someone who clearly wants to take his or her leave.

Open gestures and body movements can be a useful way of communicating warmth, trust and friendliness. As we saw above, they are particularly useful when seeking to persuade someone to change their mind or to pursue a course of action they might not otherwise have followed. Words may be the primary persuaders, by advancing facts and logical arguments, but the role of body language in this process should not be underestimated. Negotiators, bargainers and salesmen, for instance, ignore it at their peril.

EXERCISES AND EXPERIMENTS

1 The poker player

Observe a group of people playing poker or some other card game. Try to arrange it so that you can see at least one player's hand. Watch for gestures and body movements when a player gets either a particularly good or a particularly bad hand. Tell-tale behaviour will probably be easiest to observe when playing for reasonably significant money stakes. Alternatively, observe similar behaviour in a casino. List all the tell-tale gestures you spot, together with a count of the frequency with which each occurs. Does any individual have a particularly characteristic tell-tale gesture?

2 More everyday mime

Observe situations in which words are an inadequate means of expression. Examples might be when two people are very much in love, when someone has suffered a bereavement, is especially grateful for assistance or a favour, has won a lot of money, has won a sporting contest or race, or is deliriously happy. List the gestures that are used to communicate the feelings being experienced. How effective are the gestures and body movements used in supplementing any words spoken? Why are words alone so inadequate in many such situations?

3 Sign languages

Using whatever sources are available to you (the local library, practitioners you happen to know, or any TV programme you have seen, for instance), find out something about deaf-and-dumb language or American Indian sign language. How many of the signs are self-explanatory? How many might be useful when communicating with someone who does not speak your language?

4 We never close

Practise open gestures, such as uncrossed legs, unfolded and open arms, palms-outward gestures and the like. How do others respond? How do you feel about using such gestures? You should be able to communicate with others without feeling you have to have your arms folded and your legs tightly crossed before you feel comfortable or 'safe'.

5 Male and female

Observe other people in a variety of social situations. List as many examples as you can find of gestures that are used exclusively by men and exclusively by women. Are there any exclusively 'gay' gestures? Also list gestures that are predominantly used by men or by women. What kinds of gestures appear to be used equally by men and women? What about New Men? Or Girl Power?

6 Gestural favouritism

Observe your friends' gestures. What is each one's favourite gesture (in the sense that they seem to use it more often than any other)? Head scratching? Chin (or beard) stroking? Ear pulling? Nose touching? Arm folding? Wrapping one leg tightly round another in a kind of double leg cross? Licking the lips nervously? Do you know what your own most characteristic gesture is? You could always ask your best friend to tell you.

5 | POSTURE AND STANCE

Gestures and postures are closely related and indeed at least one writer, Warren Lamb, has taken the view that they are inseparable and has explored what he calls posture–gesture merging. For convenience, however, we shall treat posture separately. There are advantages in focusing on each aspect separately, as we have already done in previous chapters, in the same way that one can with spoken languages.

Posture tends to be ignored somewhat as far as its communicative value is concerned. It has traditionally been associated with classes in deportment at finishing schools for young ladies and with walking around a room with a book balanced on the top of one's head. But it has a much more significant role to play than this. Not that deportment is unimportant, but it is only one aspect of the use of posture.

We each have a repertoire of postures that we characteristically use though these repertoires are quite limited. It is possible for us to recognize people we know at a distance from the postures they typically use. Posture can be a clue to personality and to character. The person who usually holds his body erect often has a quite different temperament from the person who slouches about with rounded shoulders.

There are three main kinds of posture: standing, sitting (with which may also be included squatting and kneeling) and lying down. There are many variations upon these, depending upon the different positions of the arms and legs, and the various angles at which the body may be held. One American researcher, Ray Birdwhistell, has produced a very complicated classification of possible postures, but some are used only in particular cultures (like the Japanese bow on greeting) and any particular individual will have a narrow range of preferred postures.

These preferred postures recall a person's past. People who have, at some time in their lives, gone through prolonged periods of depression, for instance, still stoop and sag even years after they have recovered and resumed normal lives. It may be that changing postural patterns is an important part of the process of changing attitudes and of improving the ability to establish positive, communicative relationships with others.

EXERCISE: WALKING TALL

You may already be the kind of person who regularly maintains an erect posture and, if you are, you might decide to omit this exercise. But the vast majority of readers who do not will find it an interesting, revealing and beneficial one.

The essence of the exercise is that for the next week you should walk with your body erect, your shoulders straight and your head held high. Don't stretch yourself up artificially, but don't allow your body to sag, your shoulders to become rounded or your head to hang. The easiest thing to do is to look ahead rather than down at the ground, to keep your shoulders back and your stomach in. You should not put too much effort into this, only as much as is necessary.

After you have practised moving about like this for a few days, consider how you feel. Do you feel any different? Do you feel more positive and confident? Do you feel more relaxed? Do you feel physically fitter? Do you find you are moving about a little more quickly? Do you notice more of what is going on around you? Do you find yourself thinking quicker and more clearly? What else do you notice about yourself?

Consider also how other people react and respond to you. Do they seem warmer and more friendly? Do they seem more ready and willing to interact with you? Do you find yourself getting more of your own way in encounters with others? Do they comment at all upon your bearing and comportment? Are there any negative responses to your more erect posture? Do you notice any other changes in other people's behaviour towards you?

As in previous exercises, you should note or record as many of your own and others' responses to these questions as possible.

Exercise review

If you have not been accustomed to moving around with an erect posture, you will probably have noted a number of things from this exercise. It is quite likely, though not inevitable, that you will be beginning to feel rather more positive and confident in your everyday activities. It is possible that, paradoxically, although you have been trying to maintain an erect posture, which may well have required a little effort and concentration at first, you have found your new posture more comfortable and relaxing. You will probably feel fitter physically and will tend to be walking a little more quickly, without feeling that you are hurrying.

You will certainly be noticing more of what is going on around you and you may find yourself reacting more quickly. Your thinking generally may be clearer and more precise, as well as faster. Any other changes you have noticed in yourself should mostly be welcome and positive ones.

As far as the reactions of others are concerned, you should be finding that they appear to be responding to you with greater warmth and friendliness and that they are more willing to interact with you. You might find that your point of view is accepted more readily and more often (this may partly be because an erect posture is commonly used by naturally dominant individuals). Any comments that have been passed on your newly assumed posture will tend to be complimentary rather than derogatory. If there have been any negative comments, they may have been that you were slightly overdoing the posture. This is something you need to guard against in carrying out exercises like this.

Mind-reading through posture

No one wants to suggest that you can tell the details of what someone is thinking simply from observing their posture. It is possible, though, to tell a great deal about their state of mind; whether they are hopeful or depressed, confident or shy, dominant or submissive, and so on. For instance, those who are feeling hopeful, confident or dominant will generally adopt more erect body postures than those who are feeling depressed, shy or submissive. Posture observation is thus a useful activity, particularly before an encounter begins, as it can guide us in determining what might be the most productive approach to make to another person. Postures also have the advantage that they can be accurately observed at some distance, unlike, for example, facial expressions, where a greater degree of proximity is necessary.

Positive attitudes towards others tend to be accompanied by leaning forward, especially when sitting down. Negative or hostile attitudes are signalled by leaning backwards. An unsympathetic attitude towards another person can be shown by arms folded across the chest. If the arms are held loosely down by the sides of the body, this is usually interpreted as openness, accessibility and a general willingness to interact.

Like other aspects of body language, postures have patterns and thus contain an element of predictability. One psychiatrist has found that a patient can adopt a particular posture every time he talks about his mother and a quite different one every time he talks about his father.

It has been found that, when people are standing around talking in groups, those who are really 'in' the group have quite different postural patterns than those who are not quite so favoured. Outsiders typically stand with the weight on one foot, whereas insiders will lean forward a little with head tipped forward.

Albert Mehrabian, of whose work we shall be learning more shortly, made some interesting discoveries about posture. A relaxed attitude in an encounter, for instance, is signalled by asymmetrical arm and leg positions, a sideways lean, loosely held hands and a backwards lean of the body. This posture is most frequently used when an individual regards others present as being of equal or lower status to himself. It is used more by a man in the company of women. Less relaxed postures are used when the others present are disliked (see also page 63).

Probably one of the most interesting of Mehrabian's findings (for men, at any rate) is that women, when sitting, adopt an open-arm posture in the presence of someone they like. If the arms are folded across the bosom, this indicates lack of relaxation and usually accompanies indifference or dislike.

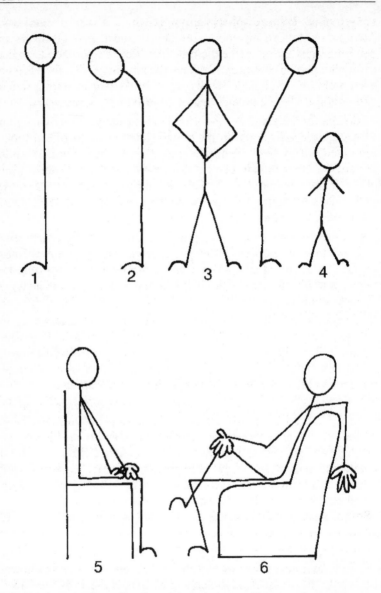

Figure 5.1 What do these postures tell you about the people concerned?

I'm the king of the castle

In the signalling of status, threat and aggression – in a sense all increasingly extreme versions of the same behaviour – posture has an important role to play. At its simplest, high status can be signalled by an upright posture and its opposite, submissiveness and humility, by a slouch or a generally sagging posture.

Equality of status is often indicated by matching postures – that is, the participants in an encounter show remarkable similarity in the postures they adopt. If one person stands with his hands in his pockets, the other will, too. If one sits leaning back in a chair with one leg crossed over the other, with the ankle lying across a knee in an open leg-cross, then the other person will echo this posture.

Lower status is often shown by bowing the head, closed body positions (as if to protect oneself from attack) and holding the body to make it appear smaller (and presumably therefore less of a threat) than it actually is. It is as if people of lower status want to show the world that they are smaller, weaker and more defensive than their higher status brothers and sisters.

Where high status is indicated by an upright posture with the head held high it may be that, as if to show that this high status is not necessarily a threat, the hands will often be clasped behind the back. But the threat may not disappear altogether, for the head may be held with the forehead out in front (as if the individual is threatening to butt anyone who seriously challenges his position).

Aggression and threatening behaviour normally consist of a progressively exaggerated exhibition of high status or dominant behaviour. Hands may not be held behind the back, but may be held by the side with the fists clenched in readiness. And the forehead (or sometimes the jaw) may jut out more obviously.

Sometimes, however, a relaxed posture can have an aggressive purpose, especially in contexts where an upright posture would be expected (as in a disciplinary interview). Extreme relaxation of posture may be used to signify a rejection and total lack of respect for authority. Nevertheless, it is mostly common for posture to be tense both when threatening others or being aggressive towards them and when being threatened or at the receiving end of aggressive behaviour. Certainly, it is more usually the case that a tense individual is more to be feared than a relaxed person. Someone who is tense is clearly closer to taking physical action than someone who is relaxed.

I'm inclined to like you

Albert Mehrabian has made some interesting discoveries about the relationship between posture and liking. For instance, he found that when people like each other they tend to lean towards each other. This appears to be the case whatever the degree of liking, from mild acceptance of another's continued presence to the closest inter-personal intimacy.

A sideways lean when seated was found to be an index of relaxation and moderate degrees of lean showed friendliness. Men showed the least sideways lean and the least body relaxation with other men whom they disliked intensely. Women, however, showed the most sideways lean with other men and women whom they disliked. In women who were sitting down, placing of the arms and legs in an open posture conveyed liking for older and younger individuals but not for those of the same age. An arms akimbo position was much more likely to be used in the presence of individuals of lower status than in the presence of those holding higher status. This was also true for a raised head, relaxed hand and body postures, and sideways lean when seated.

Sexual invitation can be indicated by posture. Women may lean forward and bring their arms closer in to the body so that this presses their breasts together and deepens cleavage. Men, especially younger men, typically stand with the thumbs hooked over trouser waists or hooked into trouser pockets, with the fists very loosely clenched.

Ekman and Friesen found that, whilst facial expression gave more information about emotions, posture showed the degree of intensity. Other researchers have found that postures say a lot about a person's emotional state. The extremes can be seen in the postures of some mental patients. Depressives droop, are listless, sit brooding and looking downwards. Manics (the opposite of depressives) are alert, erect and their bodies show a high degree of tenseness in posture.

Some of these findings are difficult to interpret. Why, for example, should open postures when used by women indicate liking in the presence of older and younger people but not for those of the same age? It is not clear. It may be that there is an undiscovered defect in the experimental procedure. Certainly with posture, as with all other aspects of body language, continuing research is necessary to explain and establish any unexpected findings and to clarify those which seem to defy a proper explanation at present.

Nevertheless, it seems to be pretty well established that leaning forward with a relaxed posture is one way of showing someone that you like them. No need to bend double, of course: here, as elsewhere, balance is necessary (in this case literally as well as metaphorically).

Posture research

In addition to the findings that have already been reported, posture research has unearthed some other and not immediately obvious discoveries. One such is the extent to which participants in an encounter copy each other's postures. This postural echo means that if one person clasps his hands together or crosses his legs or folds his arms, others will follow. The tendency is especially marked where there is a high degree of rapport between the individuals concerned.

Conversely, there can be postural conflict, in which people deliberately adopt postures different from those assumed by others. This is usually done to emphasize differences and to place 'distance' between one person and another. Postures can also be used to mark the boundaries of an interaction. Arms may be placed in such a way, and legs stuck out, to show that this is a group and that intruders will not be welcome. Sometimes it may be done so that, short of physical violence, it is impossible to enter a group. This can be particularly noticeable in pubs and cafés frequented by groups of young people.

Albert Scheflen observed that in quasi-courtship behaviour postural shifts occurred which were similar to those seen in real courtship sequences. This behaviour occurs commonly when people of the opposite sex are conversing. Grooming (stroking the hair or straightening the tie) is followed by the adoption of an appropriate positioning (face to face or side by side). In the subsequent conversation, breasts may be stuck out, pelvises rolled, hands placed on hips and other sexual postures adopted, even though the situation is not an overtly sexual one. This may be so marked that there may even be verbal disclaimers from one or other person to indicate that the behaviour is not meant seriously.

Other shifts in posture are used to mark stages in conversation. For example, when there is a change in topic from a general subject to a more intimate or private one, there will also be a change in posture which brings participants closer together. There are even shifts in posture during sleep to mark the stages, such as moving from dreamless sleep into the kind of REM (rapid eye movement) sleep which accompanies dreaming. These shifts in posture are so regular that they are predictable and follow a pattern. Understandably, it is an area which has received a good deal of research attention.

An interesting area of research into posture (and, indeed, gesture) is associated with its absence – or, rather, with the absence of these patterns. It seems to be the case that those few amongst us who possess what one may call 'presence', or an air of distinction and high status, exhibit very few changes in posture and use very few gestures. This low peripheral movement, as it is termed, is the kind of behaviour that can readily be observed on TV when members of royalty and when senior statesmen are being shown.

Research has also been carried out into the relationship between posture and personality factors. Folded arms in a kind of self-wrapping posture indicate withdrawal and a desire for self-protection, especially of the breasts. It is, therefore, more common among women than men. Talking with the shoulders held in shrug position and with the palms facing outward indicates helplessness and inadequacy.

Exaggerated postures

Posture reflects a person's body image (compare the postures of two young girls, one of whom is ashamed of her breasts and the other of whom is proud of them) and has an important part to play in self-presentation (one can use posture as an aid in deliberately projecting a particular personality). Posture has always, therefore, been of considerable interest – as have gestures – to those involved in dramatic performance and public speaking. In these activities, posture frequently has to be exaggerated in order to be easily observable by an audience. It is useful, then, to observe actors and politicians because this can help in identifying the postures (and, indeed, other aspects of body language) which are appropriate or inappropriate to various situations.

Exaggerated postures can also be observed in the behaviour of those who are drunk. Here, though, there is little to be gained through emulation since most people will react negatively to the behaviour of drunks. They will not wish to be associated in any way with them. Witness the words of the old song:

> You can tell the man who boozes
> By the company he chooses,
> And the pig got up and slowly walked away.

Adopt the posture of one who is drunk and you will soon find out who your friends are.

EXERCISES AND EXPERIMENTS

1 Have you the inclination?

Next time you are sitting talking to someone you know well, try leaning slightly towards them. You should notice that this encourages them to talk more, makes them feel you are more interested in what they have to say and generally results in a more satisfactory encounter. Then, on an occasion after that, try leaning back and away from them. You should notice that they tend to talk less, feel you are less interested in them and show signs of not being completely happy with the way the encounter is being conducted.

2 I am your mirror

Observe how, in encounters in everyday life and on TV, the participating individuals copy or echo each other's postures. Compare situations in which echoing is present with those in which it is not. You should find that, where there is evidence of echoing, the interaction proceeds more smoothly, there appears to be a better relationship between participants and the whole event looks more natural. Conversely, where echoing is absent, you should notice signs of friction, more disagreement and a general sense of people being ill at ease. If you try to use postural echo, it is important that you do it as unobtrusively as possible. If you change your posture immediately the other person changes his or hers, this will be more off-putting than if there is no postural echo at all. They may even feel that you are consciously trying to mimic them, which they will find very unsettling.

3 Sit up straight

Try sitting up reasonably straight in some encounters and deliberately slouching in your seat in others. Note the reactions of others to this behaviour. You should find that they respond more positively, with greater warmth and friendliness, make the encounter last longer and seek further encounters, when your posture is upright than when it is slouched, but not if it is too rigidly upright.

4 Who's drunk?

Observe the behaviour of people who are drunk and note how the behaviour of others changes towards them. Some people will be tolerant and even a little amused, but most will tend to avoid contact if they can and shorten it if they can't. Why is this? Speculation on the possible reasons may shed light on the importance of posture, since those who are drunk are usually unable to control their posture even with great effort. If a person is genuinely drunk it is almost impossible for them to hide it, though it may be easier if they sit down.

5 Putting on an act

Observe public speakers and actors and note instances when changes in posture appear to be exaggerated beyond what is normal in everyday life. Examples might be a politician suddenly leaning forward towards his audience in the middle of a speech or an actor deliberately turning his back on another. Why is there a need for exaggeration of posture or of postural changes in contexts like these? Try to identify as many possible reasons as you can. Some are:

■ the distance between speaker and listener is greater and exaggeration is necessary for the sake of clarity;

- dramatic performances of any kind rely upon a certain amount of exaggeration for purposes of emphasis;
- many of those engaged in acting out a role tend to be the kind of people who customarily exaggerate their posture (as well as other aspects of body language) to some extent.

6 Come on

In encounters, practise closed postures by crossing your legs, crossing your arms in front of the body, turning your body away from the people you're speaking to, and using posture to prevent others entering an interaction. Then practise the converse of these: open postures. Make greater use of open-palm posture, facing people and leaning towards others slightly. Note both how others react differently to open posture and also how you feel about being more posturally open towards others. You should find that there is a clear preference in most situations, both by yourself and by others, for openness.

6 PROXIMITY AND ORIENTATION

We have already encountered, in Chapter 4, one of the sub-disciplines of non-verbal communication, kinesics, or the study of body movements. Another sub-discipline is *proxemics*, or the study of the use of space when communicating. How close we are to people and whether we are facing towards them or away can affect the interaction which takes place in significant and often predictable ways.

Edward Hall, who coined the term proxemics, defined four zones in the use of space.

- From zero to one and a half feet (0–0.5 m) he called the *intimate zone*, in which people are actually touching or are easily able to touch each other.
- The second zone is *personal* and extends from one and a half to four feet (0.5–1.2 m) and here people are able to shake hands or are, at most, no more than arms' length from each other.
- The third is the *social-consultive* zone and runs from four to ten feet (1.2–3m). It is most commonly used in everyday encounters of a social or business nature.
- The final zone he called the *public zone* and this extends from ten feet (3 m) outwards.

Hall further sub-divided each zone into *close* and *not close* areas.

Learning to use space more effectively will help us to take an important step forward in our developing mastery of body language. We shall consider five main aspects:

- the effects of different kinds of seating arrangements upon face-to-face communication
- horizontal, vertical and asymmetric orientations
- how status is shown by proximity and orientation

■ what happens when people come too close
■ some of the ways in which we can use proximity and orientation to make interaction with others easier, more comfortable and more effective.

One interesting experiment carried out by James Baxter and Richard Rozelle illustrates the often dramatic effects of changing the distance between people when they are communicating. They selected two groups of people, one to be subjected to very close face-to-face interviewing by someone playing the role of a police officer and one to undergo a lesser degree of proximity. They called these two situations severe crowding and mild crowding.

The interview in each case was in four two-minute parts. The 'policeman' asked each person about the contents of his wallet. For both groups, the officer remained four feet (1.2 m) from the individual during the first two minutes. At the beginning of the second two minutes, he casually moved forward until he was about two feet (0.6 m) away. In the third two minutes, he moved to within a few inches with the severe crowding group, but remained at two feet (0.6 m) with the mild crowding group. In the last two minutes, he moved back to the two feet (0.6 m) distance with the severe crowding group and simply remained where he was for the mild crowding group. He was told to maintain eye contact with all his interviewees in all parts of the interview.

Those who were in the severe crowding group reacted very differently from normal when the 'policeman' was at his closest to them. Their speech became disrupted and disorganized. There was an increase in eye movements and gaze aversion. They adopted positions which enabled them to place their arms and hands between themselves and the interviewer. They often held their hands clasped protectively at crotch level like footballers waiting for a free kick to be taken and were generally much more nervous and restless when the interviewer had invaded their personal space by approaching too closely. This demonstrates the power of proximity and shows that, like other aspects of body language, we need to increase our sensitivity in using it.

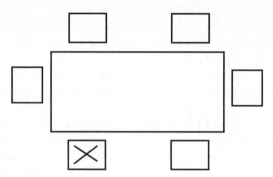

Figure 6.1 Choose a seat

EXERCISE: COMPETITION *VERSUS* COOPERATION

Figure 6.1 shows a table and six chairs. The 'X' indicates that a person you are about to meet is sitting there. What you have to do is decide which chair you would occupy in each of the following situations:

a You are going to play a game of chess with this person and it is important for you to win. Place an A on the seat you choose.

b You are going to help the person complete a crossword puzzle. Place a B on the seat you choose.

c You are going to interview the person for a job in a small, friendly organization. Place a C on the seat you choose.

Now, on Figure 6.2 place an X for the other person and a O for yourself on the seats you consider most appropriate if you were going to conduct a formal disciplinary interview.

Exercise review

According to the research that has been done, you are most likely to have picked certain positions for each of the situations posed in the exercise.

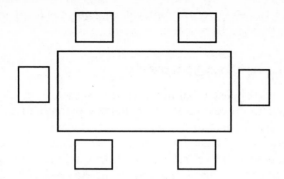

Figure 6.2 Positions for a disciplinary interview

For **a**, you will probably have picked the seat immediately opposite the person against whom you were to play a game of chess. As we shall see later, we tend to sit opposite people we are competing against. It may have something to do with the fact that we like to be in a position from which we can see everything an adversary does.

For **b**, you will probably have chosen the seat next to the person you were to help (that is, the seat to the right of the one marked X). We tend to sit alongside people if we are in a cooperative relationship with them. There is, perhaps, not such a great need to keep an eye on what someone is doing when we are not competing against them.

For **c**, you probably selected the seat diagonally to the left of the person, at the end of the table. Again, as we shall see, such diagonal seating arrangements have been shown to be particularly useful for interviewing situations.

When you were selecting positions for a disciplinary interview, the chances are that you placed yourself at the opposite end of the table from the person you were to reprimand. It is probably natural to want to distance oneself from what is likely to be an unpleasant task. It may, however, be that the diagonal seating arrangement used for other kinds of interviews may take some of the edge off the situation. Look at the exercise again and try to visualize the interaction that would take place in each possible combination of seats. You should feel that the diagonal arrangement offers the best compromise between the overly formal and the too casual. If you do not feel this way at the moment, perhaps you will change your mind when you have read through the rest of the chapter.

Seating arrangements

Where people choose to sit in the various situations in which they find themselves reveals certain predictable patterns of behaviour. But where they choose to sit may not always be the best position for them to achieve what they wish to achieve. For instance, a lecture room will tend to fill up from the back forwards. Yet, people have presumably gone along to hear what someone has to say: it would, surely, be better to occupy a seat at the front rather than the back.

Similarly, many people adopt absurdly formal seating arrangements for interviews – arrangements that can be shown to inhibit rather than encourage the very thing that is supposed to take place, that is, the fullest and freest possible exchange of information and views. Individuals who go into bars and other social settings in the hope of meeting someone they can talk to will often seek a seat in a corner or in some other position from which they can observe. These are not, however, positions that others are likely to be drawn to – far better to place oneself boldly in the centre of movement and activity: most likely a seat at the counter in a bar or at a table near the counter if those seats are all occupied.

Albert Mehrabian, whose work we have encountered before, made some interesting suggestions for those who find themselves alone in a public place, perhaps in a strange city, and who wish to leave the possibility of talking to someone else open. Fairly obviously, sitting with your back to other people present will tend to preclude such a possibility. Sitting facing may well be a little daunting, not only for the person taking up such a position, but also for the people already there. Sitting at an angle offers a good compromise. It prevents too much initial closeness and it does offer the chance of joining in a conversation at a later stage if this becomes appropriate. In fact Mehrabian suggested a zig-zag design for bar and cafeteria tables and counters which he feels would encourage such increased contacts (see Figure 6.3).

As you can see, this provides a very flexible arrangement in which groups of people can converse, while at the same time leaving it

Figure 6.3 Mehrabian's zig-zag design for cafeteria tables

open for people to keep themselves to themselves if they wish. If the seats are on swivels, this increases the flexibility of the arrangement.

In a cafeteria of the traditional design with square or slightly oblong tables, an 'adjacent sides at right angles' arrangement is favoured by people who wish to talk to each other. People who do not wish to talk tend to sit opposite one another if the tables are square. If the tables are oblong, and where there are, say, two seats at either side of the table and one at each end (as in the exercise you did earlier), people who wish to talk will sit either directly opposite each other or diagonally across the corner at one end. People who do not wish to talk will sit either at the ends or diagonally opposite each other on each side.

As we saw in the exercise, those whose relationship with each other is competitive will tend to sit facing each other. Those whose relationship or task is a cooperative one will tend to sit side by side. Not only are these positions naturally taken up by most people in such situations, they can be used to encourage the kind of behaviour desired. That is to say, if you place people opposite each other they will tend to compete: if you place them side by side, they will be much more likely to cooperate. This finding has useful implications for deciding seating arrangements at places of work and in meetings and conferences. It is interesting to speculate on what the effect might be in, say, industrial negotiations if a seating arrangement other than the traditional across-the-table one were to be used. It is also fairly clear that King Arthur's round table, giving equality to all the participants, anticipated some of the recent research into non-verbal communication.

In interviews, the positions which are characteristically taken up are not always the best available. As we saw earlier, for disciplinary interviews, people will tend to sit opposite each other and as far away as the size of the table will permit. There are still many people who will adopt the same positions in other kinds of interviews, such as job selection, counselling and performance appraisal. Yet the research that has been done suggests that, since the purpose of most interviews is to obtain or give information and opinions, the diagonal position at the corner of a table is preferable when there are only two people – interviewer and interviewee – involved. Generally speaking, it is better to have an informal setting than a formal one. Sitting in comfortable chairs with a low table leads to the exchange of more information than the kind of formal setting in which the interviewers sit along a sort of 'top table' and the interviewee sits at a separate small table in front of it.

Why do psychiatrists have couches?

Orientation is usually defined as the degree of the angle between a line joining one person to another and the direction in which the person under consideration is facing. Thus, when two people are facing each other directly, this is 0°. It has been found that the further apart two people are, the more likely it is that the angle of orientation will be 0°.

Orientation may also be symmetrical or asymmetrical. A symmetrical one means the people involved are face to face, back to back, or their angles of orientation are the same (that is, both are, say, a third or a half turn away from each other). An asymmetrical orientation is one in which the angles are different, as when one person is facing directly, but the other is half-turned away. Asymmetrical orientations permit closer proximity than those which are symmetrical, especially when both are facing. Back-to-back orientations make communication difficult because, even though verbal messages may still be understood, the fact of not being able to observe each other's body language means a large part of the total message has been removed. Mehrabian has calculated from his own researches that as much as 93% of the message in a face-to-face encounter is non-verbal, leaving only 7% for the verbal (we shall return to this point in Chapter 11).

Orientation can be horizontal or it can be vertical. In the horizontal plane the main concern is whether the orientation is facing or not. In the vertical plane, the interest is in whether the person concerned is higher up or lower down than another. Being higher up than another person, or even simply being taller, significantly affects the interaction which takes place.

People behave differently when lying down than when standing up. People lying down tend to remember more, generally. Memory recall is a negatively accelerated function of time, that is to say, more is recalled in the first few minutes. People will be more imaginative and reflective when lying down, but less receptive to action. When standing, thought tends to result more readily in action, but is less responsive to new suggestions and to close examination of a topic. Decisions are made faster and more strongly when standing. This may account for the suggestion made by at least one authority on management techniques that daily action conferences by managers should be taken standing up rather than the more normal sitting round a table. And the findings about how people remember more and are more reflective when lying down may have some bearing on the answer to the question with which we started this section.

Status, proximity and orientation

In considering positioning as an aspect of orientation, it is interesting to note how status is both conveyed by positioning and can be conferred by it. It has been noticed, for instance, that people who sit at either end of the table in a jury room are most often elected foremen: the 'head of the table' position is, then, a reality and is quite clearly associated with higher status. It has also been observed that senior people align themselves on the right-hand side of a chosen leader, which means that the term 'right-hand man' may be based on what actually happens.

Being higher up, for instance on a rostrum or simply by being taller, puts a person in a dominating position. Leaders tend to be taller and this is emphasized by the relatively few well-known historical leaders who were on the short side. However, it has also been somewhat confusingly observed that leaders tend to sit down whilst others stand.

In some interesting experiments, the behaviour of people entering offices has been studied for what it can tell us about how we signal our status to others. It was observed that low-status individuals tend to stay near the door on entering. Those of higher status approach the desk. Those of equal status will come in and sit down next to a person's desk. Friends are met by the individual whose office it is coming out from behind the desk.

Proximity and orientation, then, can be used not only to indicate status but also to seek its being accorded to us by others. Although it is not the only factor to be considered, it is nevertheless an important one.

Don't come any closer

Robert Sommer has defined what he calls personal space as that area around each of us which we do not like others to enter except by invitation or under certain special circumstances. We carry this personal space around with us wherever we go. It extends rather further in front of us than to the sides and is least behind our backs.

In crowds, we are prepared to accept less personal space than normal. One researcher has estimated that in dense crowds we have six to eight square feet (0.5–0.75 sq. m) each, whereas in loose crowds we have about ten square feet (1 sq. m) each.

Sometimes our personal space is deliberately invaded by others for a particular reason. In the experiment reported at the beginning of this chapter, the severe crowding by the interviewer is similar to tactics often used by police interrogators. American policemen are sometimes trained to sit close to a suspect, with no table or desk between them. They gradually move their chair forward during the interrogation so that after a time one of the suspect's knees is just between the policeman's knees. Such closeness, when uninvited, is almost always perceived as threatening.

Lovers will accept greater proximity from each other, but even here it is interesting to note that they almost always close their eyes when kissing. Since they approach very close and gaze into each other's eyes for much of the time, there would seem to be no logical reason why they should close their eyes for the most enjoyable part of the interaction. It may be that even in this instance some illusion of personal space, made by closing the eyes, is necessary.

Sommer's studies have shed an interesting light on human territoriality. In his studies of the kind of space people need for reasonably peaceful living, he has found that certain housing designs are more likely to lead to trouble with neighbours than others. The idea has been developed of *defensible space*. What this means is that we each need an area in which to live that we can protect against unwanted intrusion by others. If flats are too small, too closely placed, and tend to throw people together too much, this will lead to tensions, which may very quickly develop into open hostility and aggressive behaviour. However, Sommer mentions that people in a place like Hong Kong seem to have adapted to restrictions on space reasonably well. He tells us that the Hong Kong Housing Authority builds low-cost accommodation on the basis of about thirty-five square feet (3.25 sq. m) per person. When he asked what the effect would be of increasing the allowance, he was told 'With sixty square feet (5.5 sq. m) per person, the tenants would sub-let.'

In preventing violations of personal space, orientation can often be used as a territorial marker. We are reluctant to pass between two people, so facing the person we are interacting with will deter invasions of our mutual personal space. It is possible to sit at an angle in such a way as to close off an interaction to intruders, by stretching the legs out so that others will be reluctant to cross over them. In fact, the angle of orientation can regulate the degree of privacy in a conversation. People who are exchanging confidences will often turn away from the general interaction in order to discourage intruders.

If personal space is violated, people will move away from the intruder but maintain their direct orientation towards each other, as if to remind the intruder that his or her presence is not welcome and that they will resume their former positions as soon as he or she has had the good sense to move on. Sometimes, if the intruder persists in remaining, people will change their orientation away from the intruder in order to emphasize their rejection of the invasion.

A number of other interesting observations have been made of the use of orientation as a non-verbal communication tool. For instance, during arrivals and departures orientation will often take status into account, as in the frequently observed phenomenon of people backing away from high-status people before turning. This may either have its roots in the long-established tradition of backing out of the presence of royalty, or it may be that that particular custom arose out of a natural deference to status.

People who have a conspiratorial relationship with others will tend to approach from the side, literally 'sidling' up to a fellow plotter. It is surprising how often this activity can be observed at political meetings and conferences, together with the kind of turning away from the general interaction mentioned earlier.

Orientation in crowded conditions can exhibit interesting variations from normal behaviour. People in lifts, on public transport and at football matches will usually avoid a direct orientation. In situations in which the crowding is so severe that the body cannot be turned away, the head will be. This is perhaps most frequently observed in commuter trains and on other mass-transit systems where people are so crowded together they are touching. Another phenomenon often observed on underground tube trains is that people will sit rigidly, making as few movements as possible, and fixedly staring into space, avoiding all eye contact with others.

Both men and women use a direct orientation for disliked high-status men (to keep a close eye on what they might do to threaten them?) but use an indirect orientation for low-status women (partly turning away from someone who is perceived as not being very important?). It seems to be the case that where the threat potential is highest, the orientation is the most direct. It can be interesting to observe how differently people orientate themselves to the boss and to the cleaner or janitor.

When women are talking together, they will stand closer to each other and will use a more direct orientation than when men are talking together. This is but one of the many differences between the sexes in the use of body language. Such individual differences and cultural differences will be apparent in several of the chapters in this book.

One phenomenon which shows some unusual behaviour is in the case of people regarding others as non-persons. A non-person is anyone we act towards as if they were not there. Examples of such behaviour might be:

- doctors discussing hospital patients when those patients are present
- diners conversing and ignoring waiters
- people in their pyjamas or night-dresses opening the door to postmen and milkmen and feeling no embarrassment in doing so.

Someone who is a non-person or a 'fly on the wall' has a unique opportunity to observe human behaviour which is denied to the rest of us.

Making interaction easier

The more direct the degree of orientation, the more attention is normally being paid. If an indirect orientation is used, this will usually mean the involvement in the conversation is less. In such a case, there may be occasional turns of the head towards conversation partners just to show that one has not switched off altogether. If you turn your back on someone, this will stop a conversation dead. This may well be why it is often regarded as the height of rudeness to do this. Facing another and turning the head away or looking over the other's shoulder at other people present has the same effect, though it may take rather longer. In a group of three, a strange kind of divided orientation is often observable. In this, the upper part of the body may point towards one person and the lower to the third. There has been the suggestion that if this were not done the third person would feel left out.

All of this should serve to indicate that you can use orientation to invite or to avoid interaction with others. Generally speaking, a direct orientation will invite interaction. Often, you can use an indirect orientation as you approach other people so as to remove any possible stranger threat and to permit easier retreat if they indicate they do not wish to talk to you, without loss of face. If approach is allowed, you can switch to a more direct orientation at an appropriate point.

It is worth noting that mutual gazing increases with an indirect body orientation. As we saw in Chapter 1, increased eye contact will enhance the possibilities of successful interaction.

So the balance of orientation with other aspects of body language needs to be carefully watched for encouraging others to interact. It is something which can be used to help us to communicate non-verbally more effectively with others. It is thus another useful weapon in our armoury which we should not neglect.

EXERCISES AND EXPERIMENTS

1 Who is the boss around here?

Try to observe a large open-plan office. See if you can determine, on the basis of how space is allocated and how people present use proximity and orientation, who the high-status individuals are. Do they sit in some degree of isolation from the others? Do they have larger desks? Do they have more circulation space around their desks? Do they tend to sit at one end of the room or in the middle? What other territorial markers can you identify? How do the others approach the desks of superiors? How do superiors coming in from other departments behave? An ideal opportunity for carrying out this exercise would be if your observation point overlooked an organization's offices.

2 Lateral thinking

Lie down on a couch, sofa or settee and try thinking about your life as a child. After five minutes, stand up and continue your thoughts. Do you, in fact, find it easier to recall when lying down? Then, standing up, reflect on what has happened to you during the day (clearly you will need to attempt this exercise in the evening). Then lie down and continue your reflections. Do you find it easier to reflect when lying down, as this chapter has predicted?

3 Are you sitting comfortably?

If you can, enlist the help of another person or of two or three others. Conduct an interview (as if, say, you were applying for a job) in the various seating arrangements suggested in this chapter. Which seems to be the most productive? If you cannot do this, watch some interviews on television with the sound turned down, and observe from the use of proximity and orientation which seem to be progressing most satisfactorily. Are they the ones with the greatest degree of informality or those where the orientation is formal? If you can videotape the proceedings and then play them back with the sound turned up, so much the better.

4 Come and talk to me

The next time you are in a place (like a bar, cafeteria or club) where people like you habitually come to meet other people, try using proximity and orientation in the ways suggested in this chapter to invite others to interact with you. *Hint:* the easiest way will be to place yourself in or near to the centre of activity in the chosen place. You may also try placing yourself deliberately on the periphery of events and observe the differences in the ways people react.

5 Social orienteering

Study the various social situations in which you find yourself in the course of a day and try to identify which is the most appropriate degree of proximity and orientation in each case. Record your observations in your notebook or on tape. When you review them, try to do it lying down. How do your reactions compare with your observations on exercises in previous chapters when you were not lying down? Have you identified any ways of improving your use of proximity and orientation which were not discussed in this chapter?

7 | BODILY CONTACT

Touch is probably the first of our senses to develop. The baby in the womb cannot see, smell, taste or hear (though the last may not be true). Once born, touch becomes a most important sense and it is through it that much of our earliest experience of communicating with others comes. Research has shown that where babies (and other young animals) are deprived of touching by others their development is stunted, not only socially and emotionally but physically.

Touching can have a powerful effect on how we react to a situation. Even if we are touched accidentally or unintentionally, we can still be significantly affected by it. Mark Knapp reported an experiment in which, as library cards were being returned to students, the library assistant touched the hands of some in passing the card over, but not of others. In all other respects, behaviour was kept constant. The only thing that changed was whether or not touching occurred. Once outside the library, the students were asked to rate the library assistant and the library generally on a rating scale. Those who had been touched, especially the females, judged the assistant (and the library) more favourably than those who had not been touched. And this was true both for those who were aware of having been touched and for those who were not. Such is the power of even a fleeting, barely noticeable touching experience.

We use touch in many ways, though perhaps not in quite as many as we might, for ours is not a society which encourages adults to touch each other. We are too quick to place a sexual connotation upon touching and ours is not a very liberated society even now, sexually speaking. But we do use various forms of touching, to encourage, to express tenderness or sympathy and to show support.

Touching is more likely to occur in some situations than in others. People are more likely to touch:

- when giving information or advice than when receiving it
- when giving an order rather than responding to one
- when asking a favour rather than granting one
- when trying to persuade rather than being persuaded
- when at a party rather than at work
- when expressing excitement rather than listening to someone else's excitement
- when listening to someone else's worries rather than expressing their own.

One study found that 60% of people greeting or saying goodbye at an airport were touching. As one might perhaps expect, longer embraces were observed more frequently in departures than in arrivals. A number of studies have also found that touching is more often initiated by men than women.

Further findings will emerge as we look, in this chapter, at the kinds of bodily contact there are, what they mean and how we can make better use of them in developing our body language skills. It is an area in which we shall have to take more than usual care, because you cannot be closer to people (at least physically) than when you are touching them. This can make it dangerous to make mistakes. But we should still find that we can identify ways of using bodily contact to better effect.

EXERCISE: WHO'S TOUCHING WHO?

Using drawings like those in Figure 7.1, in which the body is divided into various parts, conduct a brief survey amongst your friends and acquaintances to see where they allow other people to touch them. Try to ask an equal number of males and females. Ask them to identify the parts they would expect to be touched by their mother, by their father, by a same-sex friend, and by an opposite-sex friend. Record the responses on the figures by means of tallies (see page 86 for example). Make larger drawings of your own if this will help.

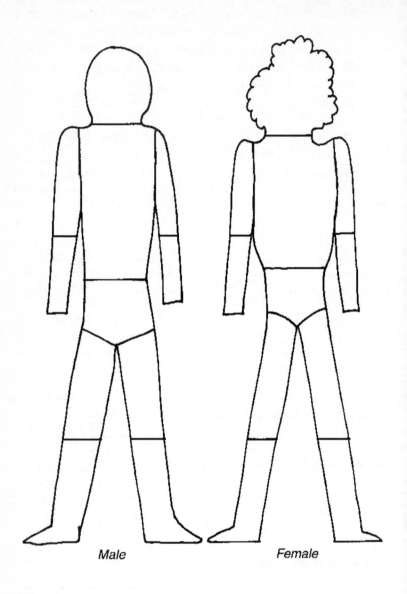

Male   Female

Figure 7.1 Where are you allowed to touch?

Exercise review

This kind of research was first carried out by Sidney Jourard and has been conducted by many other people since. The results are nearly always pretty much the same. A typical set is given in Figure 7.2 and you should compare your own findings with them. As you can see, most people (except, perhaps, homosexuals) allow much more touching of most parts of the body by opposite-sex friends than by anyone else. The exception is the amount of touching of certain parts of the body permitted to mothers. Why do you think the same amount is not permitted to or expected from fathers? Why is there such a difference between same-sex friends and opposite-sex friends? Is the reason purely sexual? You might like to speculate on the answers to these questions as no one really knows the answers.

Bodily contact and touching

Haptics is the name often given to describe touching behaviour. But it might be worthwhile making some distinctions between bodily contact and touching. In the main, bodily contact refers to actions which are accidental, unconscious and made by any part of the body. Touching implies that the actions are deliberate, conscious, and made primarily by the hands. The terms are not clearly defined in this way, however, in the literature on body language and perhaps it is in any case too fine a distinction for our purposes here. We shall use both terms, but usually touching will carry the connotation of a more active involvement of the person doing the touching.

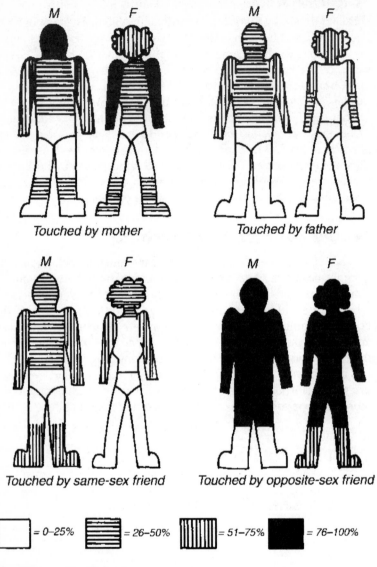

Touched by mother

Touched by father

Touched by same-sex friend

Touched by opposite-sex friend

☐ = 0–25%   ▤ = 26–50%   ▥ = 51–75%   ■ = 76–100%

M = Male   F = Female

Figure 7.2 Where people touch

Several kinds of contact have been identified. Michael Argyle tells us that some of the following are most common in Western cultures:

Type of touching	Parts of the body involved include
Patting	Head, back
Slapping	Face, hand, bottom
Punching	Face, chest
Pinching	Cheek
Stroking	Hair, face
Shaking	Hands
Kissing	Mouth, cheek, hand
Licking	Face
Holding	Hand, arm
Guiding	Hand, arm
Embracing	Shoulder, body
Linking	Arms
Laying-on	Hands
Kicking	Bottom
Grooming	Hair, face
Tickling	Anywhere

Richard Hedin has placed the various types of touching into categories ranging from very impersonal messages to very personal messages:

1 *Functional–professional* such as a golf pro with a student, a tailor with a customer, a doctor with a patient.
2 *Social–polite* such as handshakes, hand clasps.
3 *Friendship–warmth* such as a friendly pat on the back or a shoulder embrace.
4 *Love–intimacy* such as touching a loved one's cheek or a lover's kiss.
5 *Sexual arousal* such as the mutual touching which accompanies love-making.

Desmond Morris identified twelve steps which Western couples pass through on the way to sexual intimacy. Occasionally a step may be missed out, but they almost always occur in this order:

1 Eye to body
2 Eye to eye
3 Voice to voice
4 Hand to hand
5 Arm to shoulder
6 Arm to waist
7 Mouth to mouth
8 Hand to head
9 Hand to body
10 Mouth to breast
11 Hand to genitals
12 Genitals to genitals

What the various kinds of touching mean, however, depends on several factors:

- which part of the body touched the other person
- which part of the body is touched
- how long the touch lasts
- how much pressure is used
- whether there is movement after contact has been made
- whether anyone else is present
- if others are present, who they are
- the situation in which the touching occurs and its mood
- the relationship between the people involved.

All in all, the determination of meaning for touching is a complex affair – just as complex as for any other aspect of body language.

Touching implies a bond between the toucher and the touched. It follows, therefore, that the main variations in how we respond to being touched depend on the closeness of the relationship between ourselves and the other person. There is a very close connection between touching and liking. Indeed, the Human Potential movement (originally a California-based group of social psychologists and others) believed that touching leads to liking.

Touching can lead to liking, but not in isolation from other aspects of body language. You should not assume that if you go around touching people they will necessarily like it. Far better to use other body language skills to develop the relationship and let greater bodily contact occur naturally as a part of this process.

Attitudes towards touching can vary considerably. Some people for whom various forms of bodily contact (embracing, hugging and kissing) are a normal part of family life tend to have more positive attitudes than those for whom it is rare. You have to find out through observation the kinds of contact people feel comfortable with before you increase the various forms of even non-sexual fondling. Sexual touching is a very dangerous area for everyday experimentation and, because of the possibilities of misinterpretation, is best left alone. If it happens by mutual consent all well and good, but the best advice is: when in doubt, don't touch.

You need hands

There are some reasonably safe areas in which bodily contact can be increased. In greetings and farewells, as we have already seen, bodily contact is often a normal part of the occasion. Handshakes are particularly common and, if they do not occur spontaneously, they can often be introduced without any awkwardness or embarrassment. They can take many forms, from the limpest-wristed holding out of a hand and allowing the other person to hold it weakly and briefly to the strongest and most vigorous shaking of the other's hand, which has even been known to produce an expression of pain on the part of the recipient. Most people seem to prefer handshakes which are on the firm side rather than the weak. Weak handshakes seem to be associated in men with effeminacy and a general ineffectiveness of personality. Women may get away with a weaker handshake, but even here, if the handshake is too weak, it may be perceived as being offered insincerely and reluctantly. You should remember that the purpose of a handshake is to greet someone or bid them farewell or to cement an agreement. It needs to be fairly positive, warm and friendly if it is to come anywhere near to doing its job.

Hands are also used for more prolonged holding than occurs in the handshake. Desmond Morris included hand-holding in what he called 'tie-signs', or behaviour which indicates the existence of a personal relationship. Other examples are the 'body-guide', in which the hand is used to guide someone in the direction in which you want them to go by means of light pressure on the person's back, the 'pat', in which a person is patted on the arm, the shoulder or the back, and embraces of various kinds.

The hands can be used in self-touching. Some common forms of this are stroking the chin, grooming the hair, scratching the head and rubbing the nose. Such actions often occur during moments of stress. Observe a car driver who is being 'tailgated' (that is, the driver behind is far too close for safety at the speed being travelled). Very often, drivers in this situation will scratch their heads or their eyebrows or the side of their face. If you doubt this and consider that such actions are simply because the driver has an itch, try to observe drivers on motorways. You will find a noticeable increase in self-touching during moments of tension and stress such as occur in tailgating. Do not do the tailgating yourself, though, for obvious reasons.

Hugging and kissing

There is a school of psychological thought which attributes many of our contemporary personal and social problems to the fact that, as adults, we do not indulge in hugging and being hugged as much as when we were children. If only we could get back, they argue, to a situation in which we hugged each other as freely as children do, we should all be much happier for it. There may well be some truth in this, but it is difficult to see how it can be achieved. Perhaps we could each make a start by hugging those closest to us a little more often.

The same may well apply to activities like cuddling and tickling, though once again the guiding principle as to what is possible is what is appropriate. There are, after all, those who enjoy bodily contact and respond to it readily and those who are reluctant to become involved in much touching and tend to shy away from it. People are usually put into two categories: touchers and non-touchers. There is some evidence that there is an association with gestures, with touchers preferring open gestures and non-touchers tending to use closed gestures.

Another difficulty in extending the frequency of activities like hugging and kissing is the relationship between bodily contact and status. This affects all touching behaviour. It is easy enough to hug and kiss a child, but it would be impossible to extend this to one's superior at work. It is easy enough for a doctor to give a nurse an encouraging pat on the back or to touch a patient; it is much more difficult for a nurse to do the same to a doctor or for a patient to touch a doctor. Again, exceptions are small children and also, perhaps, the very old.

Stroking and caressing are touching behaviours reserved for those whose relationship is a close, usually sexual, one. In everyday life we tend to have to substitute verbal stroking for physical stroking. Eric Berne, the founder of transactional analysis, saw such 'stroking' as wishing someone well or hoping they would 'have a nice day' as being very important in improving interpersonal relationships. Between strangers, it is indeed probably better that such 'stroking' should be verbal rather than non-verbal.

There is one activity, however, in which touching is not only generally permissible but actually encouraged. That is in dancing (that is, ballroom dancing and not disco dancing in which the participants rarely, if ever, touch). Dancing can be a preliminary to later intimacy or it can be indulged in entirely for its own sake. Those who feel in any way deprived of touching experiences can remedy the situation in any dance hall – provided, of course, that they know the dance steps.

Kissing experiences are less easy to generate because of their more frequent sexual associations. In some families and social groups, it is customary for members meeting or departing from each other to exchange a brief kiss. In others, there is hardly any kissing at all, even during lovemaking.

Don't push

Aggressive behaviour often involves bodily contact, though much aggression can be expressed verbally. According to Michael Argyle, aggression is the innate response to attack, frustration and competition for resources. Usually threat displays are much more common than actual bodily contact. A built-in appeasement mechanism seems to prevent us from going so far as to damage each other, unless provoked beyond our limits of tolerance.

Amongst children a great deal of apparently violent play can occur more often among boys than girls. Young men may often be boisterous with each other, sparring and generally indulging in horseplay. Lovers can engage in playful pinching, an activity which frequently becomes a form of sexual foreplay. Such activities may even be ways in which we can get aggressive tendencies out of our systems.

It would clearly be better if we could react to aggressive situations in the same kind of way that we react to uninvited bodily contact in such places as tube trains, where we respond to the inevitability of contact not by fighting it but by turning our heads away from the immediate source of contact. Turning the other cheek may, after all, have a practical day-to-day application.

Better bodily contact

From all of this we can perhaps extract some ways in which we can improve our performance in what we have already identified as a highly sensitive area of body language which is fraught with dangers for the careless and the unwary. We can develop a firm (but not too firm), friendly handshake which will give others some reassurance in interacting with us. We can engage in the social kiss in those situations in which it is appropriate. For deciding which situations are appropriate we have to develop our sensitivity to touch receptiveness on the part of others. Carrying out some of the exercises at the end of this chapter, just as carrying out the exercises in other chapters, will help you build up a general sensitivity to the use of all the various aspects of body language.

An old saying runs that the best way to knock a chip off a person's shoulder is to pat him or her on the back. This has more than a metaphorical application for, as we have seen, patting on the arm, shoulder or back can be a gesture of encouragement or support.

Often, this is just what people with 'chips on their shoulders' need, as such an attitude is frequently the result of being ignored or undervalued in some way. Similarly, friendly or protective arms round shoulders can be ways in which we can show people that we are on their side. You should remember that, in the right circumstances, touching can promote liking. As the study quoted at the beginning of the chapter showed, touching can also produce favourable reactions from others and is thus a means of influencing the judgements and even the actions of others. Touching is appropriate when congratulating others on some achievement or success. Usually, this is in the form of pats on the back, handshaking or hugging. Touching can often be used legitimately to attract attention, especially from someone whose attention is clearly elsewhere. It can also be used when guiding people.

EXERCISES AND EXPERIMENTS

1 Don't touch me

In a café, restaurant, bar or other public place, observe people's touching behaviour. Try to identify the touchers and the non-touchers. Are there differences in other aspects of each group's use of body language?

2 Give me a hug

The next time it is appropriate, hug someone whom you know well but who you would perhaps not think it necessary to hug in order to communicate your affection for them. Examples might be mother, father, sister, brother, wife, husband or other close relation. What are your reactions to this exercise? What was their response?

3 Who is it?

Enlist the cooperation of one or two friends. Ask one of them to blindfold you and then direct you to another person. Try to identify that person by touching their face and head only. How easy is it to do this? Get the others to take it in turns to carry out the exercise. Discuss your responses to the activity. Can you find any general rules for identifying people by touch? How do people feel about being identified in this way?

4 Shake hands, pal

During the course of a day, try giving the people you meet different kinds of handshakes when you meet them. What are their reactions? Do you feel that people prefer a stronger or a weaker handshake? How do you react to the handshakes you receive from others? What is your own preference as far as handshakes are concerned?

5 Holding on longer

On those occasions when you find yourself in physical contact with others whom you know well, in the form of handshakes, hugs, kisses and so on, try maintaining the contact for slightly longer than usual. How do you feel about doing this? How do other people respond?

8 | APPEARANCE AND PHYSIQUE

We turn now to considering the communicative value of the way we look to other people. The size and shape of our bodies and the way we cover those bodies with clothing of various kinds exerts a considerable influence over how other people perceive us and over how much attention they pay to us. These would seem, at first sight, to be areas over which we can exert little control but, as we shall see, this is not the case. Indeed, they are areas in which we have considerable scope for manipulation, without it appearing as such to those we meet in the course of our daily lives. Some aspects are completely within our control, but others are only partly so.

Mark Knapp invited us to envisage a typical American morning scene. The lady of the house replaces her night-time bra with a slightly padded uplift bra. She puts on her girdle. She puts on her face with eyebrow pencil, mascara, lipstick, rouge (or blusher), eye liner and false eyelashes. There may be many more things to do before she feels ready to face the world. The man of the house shaves his face, removes his false teeth from their overnight soak, gargles, pats on his aftershave and decides what to wear.

There is no doubt that we go to a great deal of trouble to make ourselves presentable to the world. Very few of us indeed simply climb out of bed, dress in what we wore the day before and set out to confront whatever the day has to offer. We clearly realize that the way we look makes a difference to the way others will react and respond to us.

Knapp quoted some dramatic, and disturbing, examples of how our appearance can affect others, and hence ourselves. A judge in Italy fined a German woman tourist for crossing her legs in such a way as to bare a thigh whilst she sat drinking coffee with friends at a roadside café. A research psychologist found that a woman hitch-hiker could double the number of lifts she was offered by adding two inches of padding to her bust. A nineteen-year-old girl with a face so deformed that people were repelled by it committed a crime in order to be arrested. The judge ordered plastic surgery for her. He felt a change of appearance would lead to a change of behaviour and reduce antisocial tendencies.

Appearance and physique may not always make the difference between honesty and a life of crime. Appearance does, however, need to be taken seriously if we are to further our mastery of body language.

EXERCISE: A COMPLETE CHANGE OF CLOTHING

The next time you go out socially, dress in an entirely different way from the way in which you usually dress. If you are in the habit of wearing a suit and tie, dress very casually, or vice versa. What differences do you notice in the way your friends react? In the way strangers react? Do men react differently from women? How do you feel about dressing differently? Does it make you feel uncomfortable or is it a liberating experience?

Exercise review

You should have found, at the very least, that you can change your appearance and other people will tolerate it even if they may comment adversely. At the best, you may well have found that a different style of dress would be better for you in future because it will enable you to interact more successfully with others. Clothes can give confidence if they are selected carefully with an eye to what is most appropriate. Timid people often have a tendency to dress perhaps a little too conservatively. If this exercise has persuaded a few to be a trifle more adventurous, it may very well have served a particularly useful purpose.

If you deviate from clothing norms at work, you could well receive critical comments, not only from your colleagues or workmates but also from your superiors. Many companies have a 'dress code'. Your boss may even tell you to go home and change into your normal work clothes. However, if you receive no adverse comment at all, you either work in a liberal environment or in a job where choice of clothing does not matter. If this is the case and you always dress in the same way, you now know you can be more varied in your choice of attire.

First impressions

As we saw in the last chapter, our first contact with other people is 'eye to body'; that is, we look first at their bodies before we establish eye contact. Exceptions there may be to this, but in general it is true. This means that the first things we usually see are the clothes they are wearing, and from them we make certain judgements.

Clothes may, in moderate and colder climates, be necessary for protection and may be required by the culture on grounds of modesty, but they still have considerable communicative value. They reveal something about our income, our status, our occupation, our personality, and many other things. People can tell a great deal about us simply from our choice of clothes from the great variety available. Even things 'thrown on' in the most hurried and casual manner still speak volumes. It is no good our trying to give an impression to others, say of wealth or of fashion-consciousness, unless our clothes support what we say. They will certainly give our game away.

Clothes can, of course, be categorized in many ways, but one basic distinction is whether they are formal or informal. Formal can include more than tuxedos or dinner jackets. It includes uniforms of various kinds and even the business executive's suit. School uniforms may be regarded as formal. This reflects changes in society.

At one time not so long ago lounge suits were thought of as informal, and invitations to functions which say 'dress informal' may still mean you will be frowned on if you turn up in well-worn sweater and jeans. However, in an everyday context, informal dress usually now means just this and also includes anoraks, open-necked shirts, all kinds of trousers or shorts, and so on. Women may now also wear these things as well as jumpers and skirts and dresses of an astonishing variety.

Generally speaking, formal clothes are more common at work and informal at play, but we tend to choose what we shall wear on the basis of what is comfortable, what covers our bodies with appropriate modesty, or what displays our bodies so as to convey to others the image we have of ourselves. We also have to take into account the prevailing 'rules' about what is acceptable. Many clubs and even bars and restaurants will not serve you unless, if you are male, you are wearing a jacket and tie. The converse can be observed on continental beaches in summer when a woman may feel overdressed if she wears anything more than a bikini bottom.

Fashion is particularly influential in determining what young people will wear, though nowadays there is no single fashion to follow. So fashion is no longer the restricting influence over choice that it once was. Jewellery and other adornments complete the effect of the clothes.

We must not neglect the effect of body shape within the clothes. Our bodies may determine more than the size of shirt or dress. Advice to the overweight, for example, often recommends darker colours for the lower part of the body and lighter ones for the top, vertical stripes rather than horizontal, and so on. It appears that, with care, even fat can be disguised and so promote the possibility of achieving a better first impression.

You've gotta have style

Clearly, then, since how we dress can be manipulated, it can become an important element in our communicative style. Our choice of clothing tells others who we are, or at least it tells them how we see ourselves. It identifies our uniqueness or, if we are wearing a uniform, our similarity to others. It shows how we view our own personality. This is often conveyed by colour, where more introverted people will choose quieter or drabber colours and the more outgoing will go for brighter and even contrasting colours. Our clothing will show our age and sex, usually, and may even give hints about our social class or status and our occupation.

How much we communicate to others through our choice of clothing can depend on how much we want to communicate. This may be limited by our physique. It is difficult to dress as an international jet-setting playboy if you are fifty years old and weigh eighteen stone (250 lb; 114 kg). It may also be affected by our mood at the time – sometimes we may wish to be flamboyant (say, at a fancy dress party) and sometimes to merge with the crowd. How often all these factors change will influence how often we change our clothing, quite apart from considerations of personal hygiene. Some people seem to wear the same sweater and jeans for ever; others go through several changes a day.

Appearance thus gives some useful clues as to what people we are meeting for the first time will be like. That is why salesmen and public relations officers take so much trouble to be smart in appearance. Sometimes they overdo it and come over as too smooth, too bland, too ingratiating. They go over the top and become Uriah Heeps. The trick is to go only so far as convention dictates and to avoid too many extra touches like buttonholes, breast pocket handkerchiefs, too much aftershave and so on.

Some interesting studies have even shown that the extent to which students will accept what a teacher says is affected by his or her appearance. Those who dress reasonably smartly and conventionally are more likely to be taken as experts in their subject than those whose dress is casual and too informal. Most teachers seem to be unaware of this and place a relatively low value on appearance.

Sometimes we need to be able to set aside appearance and physique and see through to the real message being communicated. We must not allow the medium to become the message. What is being communicated is more important than how, if only we can get through to it. However, this is not as easy as it sounds. Even juries are influenced by appearance. Well-dressed, attractive young women get lighter sentences, according to the research, unless their crime was one in which their appearance was an asset to them, as in blackmail or confidence trickery.

Sorting the men from the women

Even in an age in which sex equality is being actively sought and 'sexist' comments and views are frowned upon, the differences in the appearance and physique of men and women are inescapable. Inevitably, since they exist, they affect the ways in which we respond to each other non-verbally. We would be less than fair to ourselves here if we ignored them.

Men tend to be taller and heavier than women. They are generally stronger and able to carry more. They have longer legs and larger feet in proportion to the rest of their bodies. They run faster, are better throwers, and are better long distance runners. They have broader shoulders and longer arms, bigger chests, lungs and hearts, stronger skulls and sturdier jaws. They are thus better protected against physical attacks. They also have deeper voices, are hairier (though they often become bald in later life) and have a greater tendency to develop a pot belly.

You might think all this would make it an easy matter to tell men and women apart. But this is not necessarily so. Recent confusions have been created as a result of an increased use of make-up by men and a trend for women to wear the same clothes as men.

Still there are ways in which even women in men's clothing can be identified as female. There are certain areas of the anatomy to which we can look for clues: the face, for instance, for women do not grow beards. Women generally have a wider pelvis, resulting in what Desmond Morris called the 'crotch gap', a sensible natural provision for their role as child bearers. They have slender waists and thicker thighs. Their navels are deeper and their bellies longer. The breasts usually protrude. They have rounder bottoms and have more of a hip sway when walking.

One might perhaps ask why we need to be able to detect sex differences. In many everyday encounters, it is true, the sex of the participants is not really important. In an advanced industrial society, the roles of the sexes are to a large extent interchangeable; it is only when it comes to courtship and mating that the differences become essential.

We might, in passing, consider two questions:

1 Why are female impersonators so funny? Some would doubt that they are, but for those who find them amusing part of the answer lies in the fact that they often exaggerate female characteristics by making-up too heavily, over-dressing and having larger than normal artificial busts. Perhaps they are also a sign that our culture is still a fairly sexist one.

2 Is there a 'gay', or homosexual, appearance and physique? This is becoming more difficult to answer. It used to be that gay men had slighter builds and adopted characteristically female postures and gestures even

when they did not actually dress in women's clothes. Gay women used to wear men's clothing or clothing that had a distinctly masculine appearance to it. Nowadays, these distinctions are less pronounced. This may be an indication that our sexist society is becoming less so.

Body shape and size

It is easier to change your appearance than your physique, but some changes can be made. It is fashionable today to be slim and women more than men go to great lengths to reduce their body size by dieting. Men tend to try to achieve a similar result by means of exercise, such as jogging.

There are those who find such behaviour faintly ludicrous. Yet there can be good reasons for attempting to change, or even appear to change, the shape and size of your body. It changes people's perceptions of you and affects the amount of notice they take of you. Successful slimmers often report an improvement in their social lives. Even clothing which masks fatness can achieve a similar result.

Body shapes are generally classified as *ectomorph* (thin and bony), *mesomorph* (muscular) or *endomorph* (fat). Michael Argyle reports that ectomorphs are usually perceived by others as quiet and tense, mesomorphs as adventurous and self-reliant, and endomorphs as warm-hearted, agreeable and dependent. Thus, even being fat can have its compensations.

Changes can also affect your view of yourself. Again, slimmers often report an increase in confidence and a greater sense of well-being. People who become fat in middle age can become quite depressed by the change, especially if they lack the will to do anything about it. Conversely, those who slim to the point of anorexia often have a poor self-image and also become depressed. The trick seems to be to decide on the body shape and size that is the best combination of what you want and what you can achieve, to want to attain it sufficiently strongly, and then to set about achieving it in a reasonably resolute manner. Motivation does, in

Ectomorph   Mesomorph   Endomorph

8.1   Body shapes

fact, seem to be the single most significant factor in determining what kind of change is achieved and for how long.

People change

Ray Birdwhistell suggested that we learn to be who we are: it is not something which is pre-determined and unchangeable. It accounts for the fact that the people of some regions look so much alike when it cannot be attributed to shared genes. He agreed that the set of our eyebrows, our mouth shape, our face contours and many other aspects of appearance are all learned from other people we live and mix with. If this is only partly true, it opens up further possibilities for changing our appearance.

There are changes which appear as we grow older, but perhaps we can learn to avoid or postpone some of them without going to extremes. We can often resist sagging of the features, obesity, stooping and many other changes by proper attention to diet and exercise.

People often change after a traumatic event in their personal relationships, and not necessarily for the worse. After a separation or divorce (and sometimes after a bereavement), some people suddenly become much more lively and outgoing. They may begin going to dances and socializing for the first time in many years.

One of the paradoxes of life is that older people often try to look younger while younger people try to look older. Balding men may begin to wear toupees. Young men may grow moustaches or beards because these make them appear more mature. There would seem to be nothing very harmful in such activities. If others respond positively to such changes and if you feel better at the same time, they could well have a generally beneficial effect.

Improving your image

Suppose you wanted to review your appearance and physique and do something to improve them; how would you start? The first step would be to do the obvious: look in a mirror. But also study recent photographs of yourself. Observe yourself in shop windows as you walk down a street. If you can, videotape yourself, or have someone else do it. Build up a picture in your mind and then set about making changes where you feel you most need to.

You might start by changing your clothing. If you normally dress formally, try being a little more informal, or vice versa. If you habitually wear clothes of rather subdued colours, try being a little more colourful. Try experimenting a little with different kinds of clothing. If you shop carefully, it need not be an expensive experience.

You might change your hairstyle. If you are completely bald, you could wear a toupee. Many modern ones are scarcely detectable in wear. You might change the colour of your hair. It is fast becoming acceptable even for men to dye their hair. A new look here can have a considerably uplifting effect upon your personality and general confidence.

If you are overweight, you could try slimming and taking exercise. Try it for a specified period, say, three months. It is best to consult your general practitioner about the best method for you. There is no need to enrol in expensive slimming clubs unless you feel you need to be in the company of like-minded others in order to succeed.

Pay particular attention to your face and skin. Men may try growing beards or moustaches to see what effect they have, not only on others' reactions, but also on how they feel themselves. Women may change their make-up. There are many beauty books available which contain a wealth of advice on how to make the most of what nature gave, or did not give, you.

Observe other people to see what trends there are in the various fashions. You may well see something that would suit you in the way others dress and present themselves to the world. What do your friends look like? Have you perhaps allowed yourself to grow to look a little too much like them? Have you become a bird of a feather?

There is no need to go over the top and overdo the changes. Here, as in most things, moderation is the key. What do you really want to look like? Decide that and then set about it in a determined and resolute manner.

EXERCISES AND EXPERIMENTS

1 Don't innovate, copy

Cut out a series of magazine pictures which show people pretty much like yourself in various kinds of clothing. Cut the heads off so that the clothing will be emphasized. Ask several of your family and friends to rate the pictures for attractiveness on a scale of 0 to 10. Ask them what, specifically, they find attractive when they give a high score. Make a list of these factors. Try to incorporate them into your own clothing. Are the results beneficial?

2 Endo, ecto or meso?

Classify yourself as an endomorph, ectomorph or mesomorph. If you do not fit a type easily, select the nearest one, or ask a good friend to classify you. Classify your family. Is there a predominant family type? If you are young, look at the older members especially: you might see what you will look like in a few years' time. Do you like what you see? Classify your friends. Are you birds of a feather? Does anyone stand out as the odd one? Do daughters tend to look like mothers and sons like fathers? What other similarities and differences do you notice?

3 Whose clothes are these?

For each of the following sets of clothing, suggest the age, sex, status (or social class) and typical occupation of the owner:

    a Pin-stripe suit, old school tie, black umbrella
    b Old sweater, old jeans, old training shoes
    c Flat cap, brown overall, grey trousers, black shoes
    d Tight yellow sweater, short skirt, high-heeled shoes
    e Flowing, flowery dress, a lot of jewellery
    f Glasses, white coat, dark trousers, black polished shoes
    g Sports jacket with leather elbows, crumpled trousers, old suede shoes
    h Broderie anglais white blouse, black skirt, seamed tights, black shoes
    i Sunglasses pushed up on to top of forehead, bikini bottom
    j Black ornate leather jacket, leather gloves, jeans, leather boots

Use your imagination and change the wearers around (i.e. giving a's clothes to wearer b; c's clothes to wearer i, and so on). What are the effects of doing this?

4 Asking for information

Dress smartly in conventional dress. Go to a railway station, bus station or airport and ask some members of the public for directions to a pre-selected place. On another day, dress scruffily in your oldest clothes and conduct the same experiment. What differences do you notice in the ways people respond to you?

5 Judging strangers

As you go about your daily business, observe the appearance and physique of other people. Speculate on their age, sex, status (or social class) and likely occupation. What factors do you take into account in making your judgements? If the opportunity arises naturally, ask to find out how accurate you were.

6 Who is this?

An obese old man, with the soft skin and round, dimpled cheeks of a baby, the jaw line and chin almost lost in fat, eyes and nose both disproportionately small, the mouth richly curled and holding a cigar, on his head a black homburg hat, and wearing a dark, three-piece suit.

Answer (do not read until you have decided or unless you give up – it is given backwards): LLIHCRUHC NOTSNIW.

9 | TIMING AND SYNCHRONIZATION

In his book *The Silent Language*, Edward Hall told us of an assignment he once had as a member of a mayor's committee on human relations in a big American city. He had to interview heads of departments to assess whether non-discrimination practices could be adopted. Special attention was given to arranging the interviews. Each head was asked to be prepared to spend an hour or more on the discussion.

What actually happened was that, in spite of the care taken over the arrangements, appointments were forgotten, he had to wait for long periods in outer offices, and the length of the interview itself was often cut down to ten or fifteen minutes.

What these heads of departments were doing, whether consciously or unconsciously, was using time to communicate something which they probably would not have had the courage, or the rudeness, to express in words. Time can thus be a powerful non-verbal communicator.

This aspect of body language (the alternative title non-verbal communication would, in fact, be more accurate here) is covered by the term *chronemics*, or the study of the use of time. Our interest here in the field is in what it can tell us not only about how the use of time affects communication between people, but also about how we can improve our skill in communicating by improving our use of time. We shall also consider the role of synchrony in body language when people are conversing.

Our concept of time is central to our world view. Indeed, there is almost an obsession with time in our Western culture. We place a high importance on punctuality and on keeping to a pre-determined schedule. That is one reason why, in Hall's story, keeping people waiting is a particularly hostile action. The tempo of our activities tells others a great deal about us. One simple way to impress others is to appear to be always busy with lots of meetings and appointments. A fast pace is more highly thought of in the West than a slow one. We regard slow-pace people as lazy, though they may actually achieve more than those who are forever dashing about but may be getting nowhere.

EXERCISE: FASTER COMMUNICATION

Select an activity. Any activity will do, but some of the easiest ones for this type of exercise are reading, writing letters or reports, walking from the station to the office, washing the car. Time your activity. If you choose reading, time how long you take to read your daily newspaper, say; if you choose writing, how long it takes to write a single letter or report. Then, over the course of the next week, time every similar activity (reading the paper, writing letters or reports of about the same length and so on). Each time, after the first, make a conscious effort to speed up just a little. Do not put any great effort into this, simply aim to achieve a new 'personal best' each time and see what happens. The important things are to time the activity, to try to complete the task in slightly less time and to keep a record of these times. You will also have to make sure that each task is of approximately the same size each time (a newspaper with the same number of pages to read, letters and reports of the same length, a journey of the same distance, etc.).

Exercise review

You should have found that you can speed up any activity without suffering loss of quality in performance. Sometimes the increase in speed can be quite substantial. In reading, for instance, it is not unknown for increases in speed of 100%, without loss of comprehension, to be achieved in this simple way. The average increase in speed is usually about 50%. In writing the possibilities for speeding up, or saving time, are more limited, but it should still be possible to achieve a saving of time on each letter or report of about 10%, which is a not insignificant amount of time. Similar savings should be possible in a wide range of activities, such as walking from the station to the office or washing the car.

If you have carried out the instructions in the exercise faithfully. especially with regard to timing the activity and keeping a record (say, in a notebook) of your results, you should find that it is possible to save considerable amounts of time not only in communication but also in everyday life generally.

Time and tide

One way of creating time which you can use either for more effective communication or for other activities is, then, to increase the *flow* rate. This is a concept to which we will return in the last section of this chapter, when we will look at twelve techniques for using time more effectively. What we need to remind ourselves of here, however, is the old adage 'More haste, less speed'. In our search for ways of improving time use in communication, it is important that we should avoid hurrying. Hurry can lead to error. We need to concentrate on ways that will enable us to achieve our objective without reducing performance.

Another fact we must remind ourselves of is that time is a finite resource – that is to say, there is only a certain amount of it available to us. No matter how hard we try, we cannot squeeze any more than twenty-four hours out of any day. When we remember that we have to allow time for sleeping, eating and other activities, the amount of time we spend in communicating with others is probably no more than a very few hours. It has been calculated, for instance, that the average manager spends about 35% of his working time communicating with others in various ways. Given a working day of eight hours, we are talking of a period of around three hours. Speeding up activities by an average of 50% can thus release time, which makes it possible to read three journals in the time it previously took to read two, or write three reports, make three telephone calls, and so on, all in the space previously required for two.

Time creation is thus an activity with a considerable potential for making it possible to keep pace with an increasingly rapidly changing world. That is, the pace of change is accelerating and we must either find ways of keeping up with it or fall behind. But before we examine these time-creation techniques in more detail, let us consider some of the other aspects of how our attitude to time and our use of it affect the nature and quality of our communication with other people.

Good times and bad times

We are all aware that there are certain times when we feel good and can communicate with greater ease and enthusiasm and other times when all we wish to do is isolate ourselves and avoid all contact with other people. Such feelings are often influenced by the natural time rhythms of the body. These *circadian rhythms* affect everything we do. When they become disrupted – as, say, in the phenomenon of jet lag – they can cause us not only to feel under the weather but also to make mistakes, unsound decisions and to behave irrationally. That is why travellers who are collecting a hire car when they fly across the Atlantic, for example, are advised to stay overnight at an airport hotel and collect the car after a good night's sleep when their body has had some chance to adapt to a different time zone.

Some people find that they habitually operate better at one time of day than another. Some are at their best first thing in the morning. Others are better later in the day or even at night. It does not seem to matter too much which category you find yourself in, as long as the 'larks' can do their most important work early in the day and the 'owls' can organize their lives so that the reverse happens.

Part of this difference, however, is an illusion. Studies of ability in carrying out tasks at different times of the day suggest that mid-morning is best, with the early part of the afternoon showing another peak (though rather lower than the morning's) and evenings being the worst time. Nevertheless, if people feel they are working more productively in the evenings, that may be a better finding for them than whatever research suggests should be appropriate. Perhaps it is the relative absence of distractions in the evening and at night which makes some people prefer them.

Rhythm, in the form of timing, is also very important in humour. Observations of comedians can be interesting for revealing the importance of timing. You should watch some on television and note how they wait for the laughter and applause to die down, but not out, before continuing with another gag. Those who are poor tellers of jokes often are so not because the jokes they tell are not funny, but because their pacing of the joke and their timing of the punchline are at fault.

Silences and pauses

The duration of silences and pauses can have communicative value. Short hesitations, if associated with many speech errors, can indicate that a speaker is nervous or is telling lies. A long pause can be an indication that a speaker has dried up. It can also, in conversation, show thoughtfulness and an unwillingness to be rushed for a response.

Pauses when people are speaking on television tend to be shorter than in any other medium. This may be a consequence of the editorial style which frequently dictates that items in programmes should be short so that several subjects can be covered in a single programme. It is only in chat shows, when one interviewer may talk to only two or three people in the course of an hour or so, that the pattern of silences and pauses returns to normal. In police and other interrogations, silence is often interpreted as an admission of guilt, especially if it persists. In other contexts, it may be interpreted as shyness, as a wilful refusal to speak or as ignorance of the answer to a question.

In public speaking, pauses can be used to great effect to wring either laughter or applause from an audience. In some ways, the effective public speaker uses the same kind of timing techniques as the successful comedian, waiting for applause or laughter to almost die out before continuing. Speakers at conferences will often indicate that they expect applause by pausing. This is particularly noticeable at a stage-managed political conference. It is significant, however, that it is often only high-status members of the party who can make the technique work almost unfailingly.

If you can, tape yourself giving a speech or even simply engaging in conversation with someone else. In this way, you can see how you use silences and pauses, how long they typically are and whether they occur in appropriate places. You may even be able to identify ways in which you can improve your use of silences and pauses when communicating with others.

Dovetailing in discussions

A good deal of research has been carried out by kinesicists (see Chapter 4) into how we synchronize our interaction with others. From a detailed frame-by-frame analysis of films of people talking to each other, researchers have discovered that we use all of the aspects of body language we have discussed so far to pace, control and regulate our face-to-face encounters with others. In particular, we use eye contact, head nods, body movements and gestures in a far from random fashion. Indeed, synchronizing with others produces a rhythmic pattern which some believe is necessary for successful communication to take place at all.

William Condon was one American researcher who spent many thousands of hours in the analysis of films. He discovered not only that people move rhythmically when they are speaking but also that the listener moves in time with this rhythm. Even when a listener appears to be sitting perfectly still, his eye-blinks or the way he puffs on his pipe synchronize with the words he is listening to. Much of this rhythm is not immediately obvious to a casual observer, but becomes apparent only when a film of a conversation is analyzed frame by frame.

Adam Kendon, in a study of the pattern of eye contact between two people who were conversing in order to get to know each other, found that there is a pattern of eye contact both at the beginning and the end of long speeches. As one person finishes what he is saying, he looks steadily at the other, who immediately looks away and begins saying what he wants to say. Kendon found that if this did not happen, there was often a pause before the other person began to speak. It is through rhythms as subtle as these that the whole process of interpersonal communication is regulated. If it breaks down, as in communication with certain kinds of mental patient, conversation can become impossible.

Kendon also found that, when someone begins to talk, a listener will show increased synchrony of body movements, perhaps even exactly echoing the movements of the speaker, showing that he is paying close attention. Then he may settle back and show very little movement at all until he sees that the speaker is coming to the end of what he is saying, when he will again begin to move quite conspicuously. This time, his movements will adopt the other's rhythm but will not match them. By moving in this way, he is signalling that he now wishes to speak.

It is interesting once again to watch people talking on video, with the sound turned down, to see if you can detect any of these very subtle movements which help people to synchronize what they are saying with what other people are saying. The better you can time and synchronize your contributions to conversations and discussions, the more successfully you will be able to communicate both non-verbally and verbally.

Getting a word in edgeways

If you wish to break into a conversation, it helps if you are a person of high status. We unconsciously defer to those we perceive as higher in the social or organizational hierarchy than ourselves. However, even the humblest of us will stand an increased chance of being listened to if we use some behaviours rather than others.

Michael Argyle suggests there are various signals which we can use to achieve this. If we want to say something, we can, of course, simply interrupt. But there are subtler methods. Speaking a little louder than the general level of conversation will often secure attention for long enough to enable you to begin making your point. Normal politeness will then enable you to lower the volume and be allowed to finish it. It is important not to raise the volume by much, however, because this may be seen by others as being as rude as interrupting.

Making triple head nods, especially if accompanied by verbal signals like 'yes', 'but' or 'well', can work. Normally, in listening, head nods, as we have seen in Chapter 3, are single or double. The triple head nod is thus interpreted by others as signalling something other than attention. It shows them, in fact, that we want to speak ourselves.

To prevent someone interrupting you, you can raise your voice. This acts as a deterrent, but again may be seen by others as rudeness if the increase in volume is excessive. You can indicate the same thing a little more subtly by keeping a hand in mid-gesture at the ends of sentences.

To show that you are willing to let someone else take over the speaking role in a conversation, or get a word in edgeways themselves, you have several choices. You can simply come to the end of a sentence and pause. You can finish by trailing off or saying 'you know'. You can drawl the final syllable. You can end on a prolonged rising or falling pitch. You can come to the end of a hand movement which is accompanying the speech. Or you can simply look steadily at the other person, as the research by Kendon indicated.

If, on the other hand, you are offered an opportunity to speak, but wish to decline it for the moment, you can simply nod. You can grunt or make 'uh-huh' noises. You can request further clarification of the point or you can simply restate what has been said, which will encourage others to proceed and develop further.

By using signals like these it is possible not only to increase your effectiveness in conversations and discussions with others but also to feel that you are getting more personal satisfaction out of them. Synchronization is satisfying, if you like.

How to use time effectively

It will be useful for you to develop your skill in non-verbal communication by using twelve techniques, drawn from chronemics, which will help you both to use time better when communicating and to use it better in a whole range of everyday activities. The techniques can be briefly described as follows:

    1 *Increased flow rates*. An activity (say, reading) is timed and then on subsequent occasions is speeded up slightly until a point is reached where it cannot comfortably be speeded up further. Times (and hence speeds) on equivalent activities are recorded in a notebook.

    2 *Deadlines*. An activity has to be completed in progressively shorter times until further improvement cannot be made. Results are again recorded.

3 *Flexible performance strategies.* A systematic approach to an activity is devised and used. The self-training programme outlined below is an example of a flexible performance strategy.

4 *Anticipatory scanning.* Before a task, or a stage of a task, is completed, you think or look ahead to the next and plan how to tackle it. This can be seen in many public contact occupations, such as airline check-in procedures, where a skilled operator glances periodically down the line to be ready for nervous or awkward customers before they actually reach the counter.

5 *Selective perception of cues.* This means being able to identify those cues, or key features of a situation, which are more important than others.

6 *Accurate feedback.* This is obtained from the record-keeping referred to earlier and helps you to avoid repetition of errors.

7 *Adequate incubation periods.* Some time has to be set aside to allow what is learned from using these techniques to mull over in the mind.

8 *Allowance for imaginative and intuitive responses.* When you 'just know' the best and quickest way to do something.

9 *Critical incidents and learning periods.* Essentially, this means doing things when you are in the most productive frame of mind.

10 *Timing and synchronization.* Doing things at the most propitious moments and moving smoothly from one activity to another.

11 *Slippage and down time.* Having a kind of 'reserve bank' of activities for spare odd moments or for when unexpected delays occur.

12 *Critical analysis of performance.* You have to study your records, analyse and evaluate, and see where further improvements can be made.

A self-training programme or flexible performance strategy would typically take this form:

■ Select an activity. Time it and assess the quality of the performance.

■ On subsequent occasions, use whichever of the twelve techniques are appropriate (you don't have to use them all every time – be flexible) to achieve improved performance.

■ Record in a notebook all results, assessments and other reactions.

■ After, say, two weeks, evaluate the progress made.

■ Decide whether it is worth your while to seek further progress or whether to turn to another activity to progress in.

Using these techniques should result in greater efficiency and effectiveness and the creation of more time for yourself. Time creation is, you will find, one of the most liberating of experiences.

EXERCISES AND EXPERIMENTS

1 Punctuality is the politeness of princes

To find out how the people you mix with feel about punctuality, ask them what time they would actually arrive for the following appointments:

    a A doctor's appointment at 9.45 am

    b A dinner date with friends for 7.00 pm

    c A party timed to begin at 8.00 pm

    d A meeting with your boss at 2.30 pm

    e An airline flight scheduled to depart at 11.00 am

    f Meeting a friend for a drink in a pub at 7.30 pm

    g An early morning radio interview to be broadcast live at 7.00 am

    h A blind date outside a cinema at 7.15 pm

    i A blind date in a pub at 7.15 pm

    j An interview for a job you would really like to get, timed for 9.30 am.

2 How do you spend your time?

Take a sheet of A4 paper and divide it into rectangles so that you have a space for each half-hour of the working day from Monday to

Friday. For two sample weeks, record in each space the main activity you have been engaged in. What proportion of your working day is spent in face-to-face communication with others? An example of a typical day's record is given in Figure 9.1.

9	10	11	12		1	2	3	4	5

| MONDAY | Correspondence | Meeting | Telephone calls | Writing report | ″ | ″ | Lunch | Telephone calls | Meeting | ″ | ″ | Visitor | Correspondence | Writing report | ″ | ″ |

Figure 9.1 A sample time-planning exercise

3 How long is a telephone call?

Over the next week, time every telephone call you make or receive and log them in your notebook. If you have a watch or calculator with a timer or stopwatch facility, this should be easy; if you have not, try to time calls to the nearest minute as accurately as you can. What is the average length of call you make? What is the average length of call others make to you? Which are longer, on average? Try shortening calls slightly, without in any way appearing rude to others. If you can achieve it, what are the benefits (in addition to lower telephone bills)? You should find that calls can often be shortened appreciably without adversely affecting the quality of the communication which takes place. You should also find that this is another illustration of the benefit of timing an activity. It makes you aware of what is really happening and can produce some surprising results.

4 Cutting in

When talking with friends, try using the techniques for cutting into conversations outlined in this chapter. What are the results? Do you find yourself being accorded a greater share of talking time? Do you find the experience rewarding? Have you been able to identify any other techniques for gaining access to conversations and discussions?

5 Working together

Observe other people talking, either around you or on television, and look for examples of failure to synchronize. Examples would be both people talking at once for part of the time, long uncomfortable pauses, someone not being able to get a word in edgeways.

6 Plan ahead

When you are reading, working through an in-tray, dealing with a queue of people, or serving in a bar, try looking ahead briefly to the next task or part of a task. Do you find it helpful in preparing for what is to come?

10 | BODY LANGUAGE AND SPOKEN LANGUAGE

The statistics 36–24–36 will be familiar to many people, especially those sexist aficionados of the Miss World contest. The figures 55–38–07 will be less well recognized, but they are perhaps of even greater daily significance. They refer to the proportions of the impact of a message in a face-to-face encounter which are accounted for by facial expressions, non-verbal aspects of speech, and speech itself. In other words, only 7% of the impact is verbal, the remaining 93% is non-verbal. The verbal element is much less significant than is commonly supposed.

In this chapter, we shall be concerned with the 38% which is attributable to non-verbal aspects of speech and with how that relates to the 7% verbal component. It is an area of study to which the term *paralinguistics* has been applied.

The non-verbal aspects of speech include many elements. In deciding how to interpret these aspects, we take account of volume, tone, pitch, voice quality (for example, whether it is nasal, breathy or resonant), rate of speaking, accent and stress. We are also affected, as we shall see later in this chapter, by the nature and number of speech errors.

We infer many things from the voice (ignoring words spoken for the moment). We make judgements about age, sex, attractiveness, social class and educational background. We also use vocal characteristics in judging occupations, in deciding whether we believe or trust someone, and in helping to make our minds up about whether we like someone or not. Most of us will, for instance, at some time or other have met an attractive stranger and been quite drawn towards them, only to be totally repulsed as soon as they opened their mouths and we heard their vocal characteristics.

EXERCISE: TRUST ME

Using a tape recorder, record yourself trying to convince either a friend or an imaginary stranger that you are to be trusted. You might pretend you are trying to persuade someone that something you have to sell is worth buying, that they should support you as a candidate in a local government election, or that you are talking a potential suicide down from a ledge. If you can enlist the participation of another person in this exercise, so much the better.

How do you set the volume of your speaking, the tone, pitch, voice quality, the rate at which you speak, your accent, and how do you place stress on the words you use? How does your use of the various non-verbal aspects of speech integrate with the verbal aspects or the words themselves? How successful do you think you have been?

If someone else is working on the exercise with you, you will be able to obtain this kind of feedback from them. If you are working alone, you will have to rely on your own best judgement when you play the tape back. By this stage in working through this book, if you have been doing the chapter exercises conscientiously, this should not be too difficult. You should by now be noticing some improvements in your sensitivity in using body language.

Exercise review

If you have had reasonable success in conducting the exercise you should have noticed some of the following points:

> 1 In order to inspire trust, volume should be neither too high nor too low. Trust is a relationship in which two people have an equal status. It is a two-way process. It is very difficult to trust someone unless you feel that they also trust you. Loudness gives an impression of a wish to dominate, which will militate against the creation of a relationship of mutual trust. A voice which is too soft gives an impression of diffidence or submissiveness, again hindering the establishment of a relationship in which both are equal.

2 Your tone of voice has to be neither too harsh nor too smooth. Harshness grates upon the listener and will tend to repel them. Too much smoothness can make them think they are having the wool pulled over their eyes and will make them suspicious, the very antithesis of trusting. You will also need to sound reasonably confident. It is difficult to trust someone who does not sound as if they trust themselves.

3 You need to avoid shrillness in pitch. A voice pitched fairly low so that it has a soothing quality – but not too soothing – will be more likely to be trusted.

4 Voice quality which sounds nasal or breathless is not likely to instil the kind of confidence which will lead to trust.

5 A high speed of speaking will tend to prevent the growth of trust. Fast talkers are often perceived as being just that.

6 In the United Kingdom, people tend to rate those with 'standard' accents as more trustworthy and plausible than those who have regional accents. Research has shown, for instance, that teachers with what are normally regarded as middle-class accents are rated by their students as being better at their subjects, more competent and more to be relied upon than those with 'working-class' accents.

7 You may have noticed that placing a little stress on positive words and phrases rather than on negative ones helps. However, too much use of stress will have the same effect as too much volume and will communicate an impression of dominance, or at least a wish to dominate.

Supporting what is said

Body language in general can be used to support and give emphasis to what is said. The non-verbal aspects of speech, however, have a particularly important role in this regard. Emphasis can be given to important words and phrases, as we have just seen, by increasing the volume and by placing stress on them. Emphasis can be achieved by repetition of the words with a similar but slightly stronger repetition of the vocal characteristics used. If the rate of speech is suddenly raised or lowered, this too can have an emphasizing effect. The important point to remember with all techniques to achieve emphasis in communication is that the more often they are used the less effect they have. To emphasize you have to be selective. Imagine a piece of writing in which every sentence had an exclamation mark at the end of it. Too much emphasis leads to no emphasis at all.

Non-verbal aspects of speech can be used to support the emotion being expressed. Sadness is usually characterized by low volume, solemn tone, a deeper voice quality than normal, a slow speed of speaking and a relatively uniform stress upon the words. Happiness and elation, on the other hand, are characterized by higher volume, sharper tone, a breathless voice quality, a high speed of speaking and more noticeable stress on key words and phrases.

Punctuation in speech is indicated by some of these elements as well as by such things as head nods, gestures and breaking eye contact. Pitch usually falls at the ends of sentences, except with questions, where it rises. There are usually pauses between sentences. Pauses can also occur before and after particular words and phrases which a speaker wishes to emphasize. Anyone who is not too sure where to place full stops when writing can help themselves to some extent by reading aloud what they have written to see where the marked drops or rises in pitch, followed by short pauses, occur. These will normally be where the ends of sentences are.

Speech errors

Most people find it extremely difficult, even when reading from a prepared text, to read without speech errors. As we shall see in Chapter 13, an increased error rate can be an indication of telling lies or trying to deceive in some other way. These errors can take the form of simple mispronunciations of words, such as saying 'dissidence' instead of 'diffidence'. Stuttering or stammering which is not a normal part of a person's way of speaking will be interpreted as nervousness or deception. Using 'um', 'er' and 'ah' or similar noises enables the speaker to pause for thought without falling silent and thus appearing to have dried up. Often, however, it is better to train yourself not to make such noises as silences are more often interpreted as drying up by speakers than they are by listeners. Errors may also take the form of corrected sentences, unfinished sentences, coughs, omissions and other variations from the norm.

Contradicting what is said

Errors in speech and other aspects of body language tend to produce situations in which what is said conflicts with what the body is doing. A person may be speaking pleasantly to another but their body language and especially tone of voice may be frosty. A person might tell his friends that he is not attracted by an attractive woman and yet be unable to resist frequent long looks in her direction. You might say to someone that you are very interested in what they are saying and yet be unable to maintain eye contact and may frequently look away at other people. You may say to someone 'I'll murder you' or 'I hate you' and yet may be smiling as you say it. In all such cases, it is the body language which will be believed.

This makes it even more important that you should be able to examine your own use of body language critically. You are clearly serving no useful purpose if your body language is contradicting your words at every turn. The situation is immeasurably worse if you are unaware of it.

Political body language

One of the advantages of living in a democracy is that politicians are freely reported by the news media. Their frequent appearances on television are of most interest to the student of body language, since it is here that they can be most conveniently studied. Like football matches, politicians are best watched on TV. The use of close-ups, the ability to use videotape recordings to watch a piece of behaviour over and over again, and a reasonably close-to-nature colour system all help to provide an abundance of information.

When sitting, politicians tend to adopt forward lean. This indicates a desire to cooperate with the listener in discussion. They often use more eye contact when they are speaking than is normal – not only to make them appear dominant but also to give them a better chance of controlling or regulating the interaction between themselves and their interviewers. They also try to have the last word in interviews because they realize not only the verbal effect of achieving this but also the non-verbal effect. We tend to believe that the last word on a subject should be allowed to the person of highest status present.

When they are standing, politicians use gestures so exaggerated as to put the ham Victorian actor to shame. Demagogues will saw the air wildly as they rant and rave. They will thump the table, point accusingly, raise their arms in appeals to the Almighty and pause dramatically after a particularly felicitous phrase for applause. Even quite mild politicians seem to change personality once they are on the rostrum. It is like the pedestrian, kind and considerate, who becomes the road hog once he or she gets behind the wheel of a car.

Politicians take great pains to conceal their attempts to deceive people. They have to deceive people, not because they are fundamentally less honest than the rest of us, but because they have to present policies sufficiently different from those of their opponents to command our support. They know that, once in office, they will not be able to carry out those policies without modifications which make their policies similar to those of their opponents. In other words, in governing the modern state, the options available to governments are limited. Hence, the politician who claims to be going to do things differently has a credibility gap to overcome. It is a gap which few cross successfully. Those who do make sure that they control the lower parts of their bodies, which is where the tell-tale signals will be given. It is not for nothing that the public speaking politician frequently hides behind a lectern stand or, when seated, uses a table drape to conceal the giveaway areas.

Politicians seek to be trusted. They will maintain eye contact with a frank look. They will have a firm, warm handshake. They will nod frequently when listening, as if anxious to know the finest detail of your problem. They will place a protective arm around your shoulder – and you will be outside the door before you realize its purpose was to steer you out to make way for the next supplicant. Above all, they will smile.

The major political parties train their principal spokesmen and women in how to deal with the media and how to present a favourable image both of themselves and of the party. This image is established and maintained almost entirely non-verbally. After all, the words of the policies and the speeches exist already and if they were inadequate no amount of image manipulation in the world would help. Politicians have been known to change their clothing, to change their hair styles, to soften the tone of their voices and to alter their posture and gesture pattern in the quest for a better image.

In the UK there are even differences between the parties. The typical Conservative male wears a dark suit, shirt and tie, has a smart hairstyle and polished shoes. His skin is smooth and he has the air of being well fed. His accent is middle-class and the tone confident and assured. His gestures are restrained and his posture either upright or casually asymmetrical. The Conservative female is similarly conventionally dressed and well groomed. Her voice, manner and behaviour match the male's perfectly. The Labour male, on the other hand, has less of an interest in appearance. His voice may contain any one of a myriad of accents from upper crust to working class. Posture is more hunched and gestures made with less thought for their effect. They tend to stand closer than their Conservative counterparts and they use the head cock of interest more. The Labour female is more likely than a Conservative to wear casual clothes. Her hairstyle may not be quite as smooth, but more natural. Gestures will be more like the man, as whose equal she rightly regards herself, and she makes a great deal of use of the head nod and the head cock.

The body language of minority groups and of demonstrators at such events as peace marches repays careful observation. At the other end of the political activity range is the body language of the statesman. This is characterized by low peripheral movement, restraint in upper body gestures, upright postures, restrained head movements, slight smiles in public and a measured, even pace of speech. Observe television reports of meetings between heads of states and of the United Nations and you will see how often this apparent stereotype occurs. The body language of international statesmen is becoming as standard as the services and facilities in international hotels. In fact, political body language all over the world is assuming a sameness – which is discouraging rather than hopeful. One of the problems of homogeneity is that it tends to lead people to assume that they are all using the same meaning of a word or gesture, when this may not be the case. At least if differences between people are preserved, some care is taken not to assume that an action means one thing when it might mean something else.

Laugh and the world laughs with you

Doubt has occasionally been expressed as to whether a laugh is a piece of non-verbal behaviour or whether it is close enough to being a word (as other exclamations often are) to be considered to be verbal. We shall regard it for our purposes here as non-verbal.

Laughter usually follows on from, or may accompany, smiles and grins. It can be graded from the quietest chuckle or slight giggle to the most raucous of belly laughs. Laughter is also infectious. When one person in a company starts laughing, it is very difficult for the others to avoid following suit. And why should they? For laughter lifts the spirits.

Since we are concerned here with finding ways of improving our use of body language it is worth considering the laugh as an aid to this end. You should, where you reasonably can, encourage laughter. If you have the facility to make people laugh, use it; if you have not, at least encourage those who have. As long as there is an emphasis on laughing with, rather than at, the results should be entirely positive and beneficial. All you have to avoid is an inane, pointless cackle. Friendly, convivial laughter should not be too difficult to find.

EXERCISES AND EXPERIMENTS

1 Er, ah, um

Select one or two public speakers, lecturers or speakers on television. Record the number and types of speech errors they make. Which is the one that each is most prone to make? You should usually find that nearly every speaker has a favourite speech error. 'Er' is by far the most common.

2 Party political broadcast

Watch several party political broadcasts on television and see if you can identify the favourite facial expression, body movement, posture, and so on of each politician. Compile a list of typical non-verbal behaviours associated with each party. Compare and contrast them. Which parties are most similar to each other in styles? Which are the furthest apart? Is it possible to tell what a person's political opinions are likely to be from their body language?

3 Keep still

Using a tape recorder and standing in front of a mirror, record a short talk on a subject you know well. Try to make the talk without any body language at all. Is it possible? If it is, is it easy? You may very well find this exercise virtually impossible to carry out.

4 There's a call for you

Observe people telephoning. How close is their body language to what it would be if they were conversing face to face? Which kinds of body language can be communicated by telephone and which cannot? Are any non-verbal behaviours more exaggerated when telephoning than in face-to-face encounters? Do any never occur?

Part Two
CONTEXTS

11 | BODY LANGUAGE AROUND THE WORLD

Body language, as you should be aware by now, is complex enough when you are dealing with people from your own culture, but when you encounter those from other cultures it becomes fraught with difficulties. Things can so very easily go unintentionally wrong that we shall find it useful to consider some of the principal difficulties and some of the ways in which they can be avoided.

Edward Hall tells of instances in which inappropriate non-verbal behaviour, coupled with general cultural insensitivity, can cause poor communication and can even cause communication to break down altogether. One example describes some negotiations between American and Greek officials, which had reached stalemate. Later examination revealed that the American habit of being outspoken and forthright was regarded by the Greeks as indicating a lack of finesse, which made them reluctant to negotiate. Further, the Americans wanted to limit the length of meetings and to reach agreement on general principles first, leaving the details to be sorted out by sub-committees. This the Greeks saw as a device to pull the wool over their eyes, since the Greek practice is to work out details in front of all concerned and to continue meetings for as long as necessary.

Another example concerns the use of time. An American attaché new to a Latin country tried to arrange a meeting with the minister who was his opposite number. All kinds of cues came back that the time was not yet ripe for such a meeting. The American persisted and was eventually reluctantly granted an appointment. When he arrived, he was asked to wait in an outer office. The time of the appointment came and went. After fifteen minutes, he asked the minister's secretary to make sure the minister knew he was waiting. Time passed. Twenty minutes, twenty-five minutes, thirty minutes, forty-five minutes. At this point, he jumped up and told the secretary he had been 'cooling his heels' for long enough and that he was 'damned sick and tired' of this kind of treatment. His stay in the country was not a happy one. He had forgotten that a forty-five minute waiting time in that country was no greater than a five minute waiting time in America.

Effective cross-cultural communication is so important in the modern world that breakdowns like these need to be studied for the lessons they can teach us. They also make it increasingly important that people who live and work in countries other than their own should be given training in the local body languages as well as the local spoken language.

EXERCISE: BLACK AND WHITE BODY LANGUAGE

Select five Black men and five Black women to observe. Also select five White men and five White women. If you cannot find this number, conduct the observation with as many as you can find. If you live in an area which is not multiracial, select your subjects for observation from television programmes.

Record in your notebook, or on tape, clothing styles, including colours, formality of clothing, patterns, and so on. Record as much detail as you can about eye contact patterns, facial expressions, gestures, proximity and bodily contact.

When you have collected as much information as you reasonably can, analyse it. What seem to be the main differences between Blacks and Whites in the use of body language? What are the similarities? What differences are there between the sexes?

Exercise review

It is quite possible that you will have collected a rich amount of data which will repay careful analysis and tell you many things about how different races and different cultures interact. Some of the things you may have noticed are:

1 Whites typically spend about half the time in eye contact and half the time looking away; Blacks tend not to look at the other person when listening.

2 The facial expressions of Black people are less restrained than those of Whites.

3 Black people use more palms-upward hand movements than Whites.

4 A limp stance and lowered head indicate submissiveness when used by White people; when used by Blacks this indicates that the individual has switched off and is not attending to the speaker.

5 White people do not touch each other except in greetings; Blacks do more touching, especially of arms and shoulders during conversation.

6 Black people choose more vivid colours and stronger patterns for their clothing than Whites.

Cultural differences

There is still a great deal of research needed into the precise nature of the differences in the ways various peoples around the world use body language. So far, most of the research attention seems to have focused on the Americans, the Japanese, the Arabs and, to a lesser extent, certain countries of Europe. Nevertheless, some interesting findings have been made.

In research into the use of eye contact, for instance, it has been observed that Greeks look at each other more in public places, both at those they are conversing with and at other people. In fact, they feel quite upset if other people do not show an equal curiosity in them and feel they are being ignored. On the other hand, Swedes have been found to look at each other less often than other Europeans, but they look for longer. Arabs are very dependent on eye contact when conversing. They look at each other when listening and when talking. They find it very difficult to interact successfully with someone who is wearing dark glasses and whose eyes cannot therefore be seen. The Japanese look at other people very little and tend to focus their eyes on the other person's neck when conversing.

Americans and the British tend to be relatively restrained in their facial expressions. Italians, however, tend to be much more volatile. The Japanese keep a very straight face in public and use a faint smile in private. They make more use of smiles in greetings and business and formal meetings than Europeans.

As far as gestures are concerned, probably Arabs and Indians have the richest vocabularies. The Japanese have formal gestures for such actions as summoning others to them. They extend the arm palm downwards and flutter the fingers. To suggest that someone is a liar they lick a forefinger and stroke an eyebrow. A number of European gestures have already been discussed in Chapter 4.

One contrast in posture can be seen when comparing the habit of Arabs in squatting cross-legged with the Japanese bow. Bowing occurs in greetings and farewells, and persons of lower status bow lower than those of high status. Germans often tend to have a more upright posture than people from Latin countries.

Italians stand closer to other people when conversing; Germans stand further apart; Arabs stand closer and at a more direct angle. It is not uncommon at international conferences to see Americans and Europeans retreating before Arab advances as each tries to get to the preferred distance from other people. In Japan, position is often as important as proximity and you will see traditional families walking in public with the father in front, then the wife, and the children at the back.

Latins use touching behaviour more than other races, though Arabs touch a great deal and men will frequently hold hands, something which causes amusement to Europeans. Arab females are not touched at all in public. Japanese touch each other very little in public, though they have a tradition of bathing together without there necessarily being a sexual connotation to the activity.

In appearance, some races have quite strict rules. Arab women must be so well covered by clothes that only their eyes are showing. Even Arab men will generally be well covered by clothing. In Japan, uniforms abound. Schoolchildren and students have a uniform of white shirt and black jacket and trousers (or skirt, in the case of girls). Lift-girls in big department stores wear uniforms and white gloves. White gloves are also worn by chauffeurs and private hire taxi-drivers.

Amongst various other non-verbal behaviours which have been observed is the fact that tone of voice is particularly important to Arabs. They also make a lot of use of smell and even breathe on each other when conversing, an activity which Europeans find disturbing. Emotions can be recognized from tone of voice across cultures. That is, even if people do not understand the language, they can tell the emotional state of the speaker.

Non-verbal universals

There are other universally understood examples of body language – we have already encountered some in Chapter 2, for instance. Ekman and Friesen found that people of thirteen different cultures were able to distinguish accurately between the non-verbal expressions of joy, surprise, fear, anger, sadness and disgust. There are cultures all around the world in which people smile when they are happy and scowl when they are angry.

Michael Argyle identified seven elements which commonly occur in greetings:

- close proximity with a direct orientation
- the eyebrow flash
- smiling
- eye contact
- bodily contact, even in most otherwise non-contact cultures
- the presenting of the palm of the hand, either to shake or simply to be seen
- a head toss or a head nod in the form of a bow.

Negotiating styles

Gerard Nierenberg and Henry Calero have made an extensive study of body language in negotiations, having recorded 2500 negotiations for analysis. They note the importance of proximity when trying to negotiate a sale. People will tend to buy more from someone close to them than from someone who remains at a distance; hence, many salesmen carry literature and visual aids with them so that they can approach close to the prospective buyer. If the buyer reacts by folding his arms or with some other defensive gesture, the salesman moves away until the buyer's behaviour relaxes and becomes less defensive.

Signalling a willingness to cooperate in a negotiating situation can be achieved in a number of ways. Sitting forward on a chair can communicate both interest and a desire to agree with others. Unbuttoning the jacket can signal an opening up to other people. It can also show interest in what someone else is saying. The head cock shows interest, as we have seen, so this can also be used to communicate cooperative intent.

Steepling (see Figure 11.1) is common in negotiations, especially when the prospective buyer is considering what is being offered. It can also be seen in other situations when someone wishes to signal confidence and high status. But it can, in fact, show defensiveness and weakness.

Figure 11.1 Steepling

Drumming with the fingers and tapping with the feet are behaviours to watch closely in negotiations, as they tend to show boredom or impatience. These negative reactions can prejudice the success of negotiations so some action needs to be taken to remedy them. This may involve getting the drummer or tapper to speak (most people do not drum or tap when talking).

Doodling may simply show that a person needs something else to do as well as listen. More frequently it signals boredom or at the very least a waning of interest. Something should be done to involve the doodler in discussion.

Forward lean, head cock, smiling, open gestures and postures are most appropriate for those who wish to seem willing to cooperate in negotiations. If the bargaining is to be hard and nothing is to be given away, then doodling, backward lean, frowning and closed gestures and postures should communicate unwillingness to others.

Business as usual

As we have seen, awareness of the passage of time varies across cultures. Waiting for appointments can be expected not only in Latin countries but also in the Middle East, as Robert Moran points out. In the Middle East, persons of senior rank and status should be recognized first. Arabs like expressiveness and periodic displays of emotion. Group-style business meetings with several things happening at once are typical. You should sit as near as possible to the person you would like to do business with and should talk about the matters which concern you amongst whatever other conversation is going on.

In the USA, the obsession with time and schedules means that punctuality and efficiency are important. Competitiveness is encouraged. Americans are gregarious at first meeting and are not too interested in differences in status. A brisk, businesslike approach is preferred.

Africans like to get to know someone before getting down to business and the general chat at the beginnings of business meetings can go on for some time. Time is flexible and people who appear to be in a hurry are mistrusted. Lateness is a normal part of life. Respect is expected to be shown to older people.

In China, people do not like to be singled out as unique and prefer to be treated as part of a team. Women often occupy important posts and expect to be treated as equals. Toasts are an important part of business dinners and you should prepare an appropriate one in advance. Appointments should also be arranged in advance. Long-standing relationships are highly valued and are worth taking time to establish. Personal contact is preferred to letters and telephone calls. Several negotiating sessions will normally be required, as the Chinese are another people who do not like to rush things.

In using body language in particular business situations, there are pitfalls to be avoided. Robert Moran illustrates this by dramatic examples. If you wish to summon a waiter at a business lunch in Western countries, a common way is to hold a hand up with the index finger extended. In Asia, however, this is the way you would call a dog or some other animal. In Arab countries, showing the soles of your feet is an insult and an Arab may also insult someone by holding a hand in front of the person's face.

In the USA, you can signal that everything is all right by forming a circle with the thumb and index finger and spreading out the rest of the fingers. But you should remember that in Japan the same gesture means money and in Brazil it is an insult.

We often pat children on the head as a sign of affection, but in Islamic countries the head is regarded as the seat of mental and spiritual powers. Accordingly, it should not be touched.

We scratch our heads when we are puzzled. In Japan, the same action is interpreted as showing anger. In most parts of the world, shaking the head means 'No', but with Arabs and in parts of Greece, Yugoslavia, Bulgaria and Turkey a more usual way is to toss the head to one side, perhaps clicking the tongue as well. In Japan, a person may move his right hand backwards and forwards to communicate a refusal or disagreement. On the other hand, agreement is shown in Africa by holding an open palm upright and smacking it with a closed fist. Arabs will show agreement by extending clasped hands with the index fingers pointing towards the other person.

Anyone who has to do business overseas should do a little research before going, to find out what main non-verbal pitfalls need to be avoided. It may make the difference between getting an order or not. In a highly competitive world, the businessman who fails to appreciate the power of body language in business contexts will find himself paying a high price.

What to do when you can't speak the language

Whether you are abroad on business or on holiday, finding out about the body language of the people you will be meeting is a sensible precaution. But there are one or two other things you can do to minimize the risk of causing offence and maximize the chances of having a pleasant and trouble-free stay.

You should use body language that has universal, or near-universal, currency as much as possible. Smiles, eyebrow flashes, head cocks, presenting the palm of the right hand in greeting should all help to ease you through the initial phases of encounters to the point where you can use other descriptive gestures to indicate what you want or what you wish to tell the other person.

Generally speaking, a friendly expression, an avoidance of aggressive movements and an awareness of the most obvious body language dangers will help to smooth over awkwardness and embarrassment. If this is supported by some attempt at least to learn key words and phrases from the spoken language, there will be fewer difficulties. It is often surprising how delighted people will be and how warmly they will respond if you have made some effort to communicate with them on their own terms. They will often be more willing to come forward and meet you half way. Even those who live in quite formal cultures, like the Japanese, respond very favourably when appropriate body language is matched with a few halting words.

EXERCISES AND EXPERIMENTS

1 Foreign films

Watch one or two foreign films, preferably where you do not understand the language. In your notebook, or on tape, record instances of body language which are unusual, together with what they mean (if in doubt, try to consult a native of the country for an explanation). Look particularly at the use of eye contact, head nods, gesture, posture, and so on. Listen for tone of voice, speech errors, speed of speaking, pitch and so forth. Try to watch films from, say, France, Germany, Russia, India, and the Far East to get a good coverage of different cultures.

2 Getting your own way

Select an everyday negotiation, such as deciding what the family will watch on television, or seeking permission for time off work. On the first occasion try to get your own way by using negative, closed gestures and postures. On the next, try positive, open gestures and postures. Which way is more successful?

3 Business body language

Observe business people talking in a public place, such as a hotel lobby or airport lounge. What are their most frequently used non-verbal behaviours? Do they differ in any way from members of the general public? Consider appearance and physique, timing and synchronization and proximity and orientation as well as other aspects of body language.

4 I'm a stranger here myself

With a group of friends who are willing to participate in the exercise, act as if you were a foreigner who does not speak the language. How do others react to you? What are the most useful forms of body language? Are any situations impossible to deal with?

12 | BODY LANGUAGE AT WORK

We have now considered all of the main aspects of body language and how it is used in our encounters with others. We shall turn our attention at this point to examine a little more closely some of the practical applications of this knowledge for improving our use of body language in specific contexts. We begin, in this chapter, by examining how it can be used more effectively when we are at work. The chapters that follow will consider its use in everyday encounters, in personal attraction and developing better relationships with others, and in contributing to personal growth and self-development.

The kinds of occupations in which body language is most important are those in which there is face-to-face communication with members of the public. In these 'public contact' occupations we can also, for the sake of convenience, include such activities as nursing, television interviewing, all forms of business activity, and teaching.

Of all the possible aspects of the use of body language at work which could be considered, we shall also examine its use in meetings, in indicating attitudes to workmates, in industrial relations, in motivating others and in the building up of work teams. But first, as usual, let us begin with an exercise.

EXERCISE: ANTICIPATORY SCANNING TECHNIQUES

We have already encountered anticipatory scanning in Chapter 9. Here we will develop our understanding and use of it a little further. The next time you are in a public place where people are being served or attended to in some way in sequence (for example a bar, cafeteria, airline check-in desk or supermarket check-out), study the people who are working there. Look for examples of anticipatory scanning (looking ahead to the next person or persons to be dealt with while still attending to the person at the head of the queue).

Do those who use anticipatory scanning techniques seem to be better at their jobs than those who do not? Record in your notebook or on tape the forms the anticipatory scanning takes and the situations in which it most frequently occurs. What of the people who do not use it at all? How does its absence affect their work? What else do you notice about the use of anticipatory scanning in public contact situations?

Exercise review

You will probably have noticed that it is those who use anticipatory scanning techniques who are best at their jobs. In some way, the snippets of information about people yet to be attended to, which they obtain from these brief looks ahead, enable them to change their attitude and behaviour to fit the needs of the individual customer. In bars, it can enable bar staff to serve more than one person at once – they can be waiting for the money from someone who has just received a drink, be preparing the drink for the next person, taking an order from the next person and identifying the person who will be served after that. At airline check-ins, where there is a queue, those who use anticipatory scanning techniques will, as they are attending to one person, make periodic, brief glances down the line. They will be looking particularly for nervous travellers who may need a smile of reassurance and for those who are impatient at having to queue and who will need to be treated with additional tact.

What you should now do, if your own job involves public contact with a sequence of people, is to try to develop anticipatory scanning techniques for yourself. You should find that it not only increases your personal effectiveness but also improves your sense of job satisfaction.

Occupational body language

Nursing is an occupation in which body language is important because the people nurses deal with, in addition to feeling unwell, may be apprehensive about an operation or about their chances of recovery, or may be worrying about whether everything is all right at home, and so on. They will be in particular need of comfort and reassurance.

Effective body language for nurses will include increased use of eye contact, smiling and other positive facial expressions, head nods when listening, open gestures, forward lean in posture, close proximity and direct orientation, increased use of bodily contact of a supportive nature (hand holding, arm round shoulder, light hugging, and the like), neatness in appearance, attention to synchronization when talking to patients, and the use of encouraging vocalizations ('mm-hmm', 'mmm', oh').

Television interviewers need to use more eye contact than average because of their role as listeners rather than talkers. Facial expressions should concentrate on showing interest and they should make liberal use of head nods for the same reason. The head cock will also be useful. Gestures should be kept to a minimum as these may distract the interviewee. Posture may use either forward lean or asymmetrical leaning back according to whether the dominant requirement is to show interest or to put a nervous interviewee at ease by making the setting more relaxing. Proximity should be dictated by what the interviewee appears to feel comfortable with, yet people are often forced closer together than normal because of camera requirements. An indirect orientation is thus preferable, though directors seem to prefer a 0° orientation. There is normally no body contact and most people who appear on television seem to want their appearance to be as smart as possible. This is probably because their public image will be greatly affected by how the viewing audience, which may run into millions, reacts to them. Attention to synchronization will be important and non-verbal aspects of speech will be used to keep the talk going for as long as whatever time has been allowed, which is usually inadequate for the proper discussion of a topic.

On the other hand, interviewers who wish to unsettle an interviewee will deny eye contact, be frosty-faced, give no head nods, gesture frequently even when the interviewee is speaking, adopt an over-rigid or over-relaxed posture and a direct or turned-away orientation. They will also interrupt frequently with a new question before the previous one has been answered. The same is true of some job interviewers.

Business people need a different kind of body language. Eye contact needs to be dominant rather than submissive. Facial expressions will tend to be neutral, though there will be smiles on greeting and parting. Head movements will also tend to be restrained, with head nods and head cocking being subtler than in most other contexts. A reason for this is that in many situations businessmen and women have to keep their cards close to their chests. Body language can so easily give things away, so it is necessary for them to try to control it as much as possible.

One of the most important lessons the business communicator needs to learn is to adapt his or her use of body language to that of the people with whom business is being done. What was said in the last chapter about differences according to culture should be of particular interest.

Other occupations have their special requirements. Receptionists need pleasant facial expressions, plenty of eye contact and a greater attention than usual to appearance. Shop assistants need to appear smart, but not necessarily stylish, and they also need to use smiles, an upright posture and, if they are dealing with sequences of people, anticipatory scanning techniques. Salesmen need to use plenty of eye contact, head nods and head cocks when customers are indicating their needs, and close proximity and bodily contact where this can be achieved without awkwardness and embarrassment. They also need to present a smart and conventional appearance.

Being a pop star is not normally regarded as an occupation, yet pop stars often work a lot harder than the rest of us. What looks like pleasure to us can frequently be quite arduous. It's not all tinsel and glitter in show business! Their body language contains prolonged eye contact with the audience, often done in a deliberately flirtatious manner. Facial expressions, both on and off stage, tend to be exaggerated. Smiles are broader and scowls more fearsome. Head movements also become more obvious and dramatic. Appearance is usually unconventional and may even be bizarre in the extreme, with heightened make-up (even on men) and outrageous hairstyles. These changes in appearance then filter down into society itself. Life imitates art.

One occupation in which mastery of body language is especially important, not least because of its influence over the young and their development, is teaching. Teachers can use body language to often devastating effect. On the basis of the research into non-verbal communication, a profile of effective teacher non-verbal behaviour can be offered. In general terms, teachers should be friendly, warm and rewarding. They should be able to make contact with all members of a group of students. They should be confident, well organized and emotionally stable. Attentiveness to student responses and contributions is important, as is avoiding appearing to ridicule or be sarcastic, hostile, angry or arrogant. Like many others, teachers need to be aware of cultural differences in the use of body language.

This kind of behaviour can be promoted non-verbally if teachers are aware of restrictions on bodily contact, if they are generally sensitive to students' non-verbal indications of appropriate proximity and respect their personal space. They should use a relatively upright posture to indicate their dominant role in classroom interaction, but use forward lean to show attentiveness. They should adjust their orientation to suit the competitive or cooperative nature of particular tasks in class. Expressive gestures should be used to support what is said, as well as head nods to reinforce, reward and encourage others to speak.

Smiles help to provide reassurance and indicate liking and approval, as well as showing willingness to interact. All facial expressions should help to present an appropriate self-image and to obtain positive responses from others. A high level of eye contact will usually be fitting, though it should be reduced if students exhibit signs of discomfort. It will mainly be used to obtain and provide feedback during classroom interaction. Stress, tone, pitch, volume, rate of speech and timing of utterances will all be varied to suit the situation. Speech errors and hesitations should be reduced as far as possible and pauses should be used to retain students' attention, for emphasis and to encourage student contributions. Appearance can be important in determining whether students accord credibility to what a teacher says and thus needs to be taken into account. Formal dress may not be necessary, but an over-casual style will tend to reduce student ratings of academic competence.

Teachers may argue that how they dress in no way affects their ability. This may be true, but the evidence shows that students are influenced by this factor in forming their opinions about who are good teachers and who are not. Teachers who prize their standing with their students cannot afford to ignore it.

The effective use of meetings

Body language can be used in meetings to indicate a wish to speak by leaning forward or by raising an index finger. When speaking, eye contact with the chairman can help to 'keep the floor'. Where this is assured, eye contact with other members of the meeting in sequence will help to retain attention and provide feedback on how the points that are being made are being received. Facial expressions will indicate attitudes to the topic, but may also be varied in order to lend expressiveness to what is being said. The same may be said of gestures, though there is more scope for expressiveness when standing than when sitting down. Sensitivity to timing and synchronization will enable someone who wishes to speak to cut in just as the previous speaker is finishing, without interrupting, but just ahead of others who may be trying to get in.

It is worth studying meetings to see the individuals who succeed most frequently in getting the floor and how they do it. If they do not use high volume or interruptions, it is usually because their timing is just fractionally sharper than that of their colleagues.

The one person who needs effective use of body language most is the chairman. Non-verbally, he or she can achieve many things. He can prevent someone from speaking if he wishes simply by denying eye contact and looking at others to show it is their turn to speak. His facial expressions can show approval or disapproval of what is being said and thus help to control the direction the meeting takes. Often, speakers will hesitate before speaking against the wishes of someone who has been accorded high status by being placed in the chair. The chairman can use head nods to encourage someone to keep on speaking or can deny them to deter them from continuing. He or she can gesture to keep people quiet or to get them to speak or can turn away from those who are saying things he does not agree with. So much for the impartiality of the chair. In fact, because of the influence of non-verbal factors the neutral chair is virtually a myth. Whether the chairman wants to or not, he or she is almost bound to give their true feelings away, unless unusually skilled in the use of body language.

Careful use of body language can, then, save a lot of effort in trying to be heard. It is surprising how often a chairman will turn to someone and actually invite them to speak if their facial expression, for example, shows that they disagree strongly with what is being said. Being invited is always better than gatecrashing.

Attitudes to workmates

By our use of all the aspects of body language, we reveal to those we work with our feelings about, and our attitudes towards, them. Denial of eye contact, a frosty face, a turned-away orientation, all betray a negative attitude. Frequent smiling and laughter, open gestures, relaxed postures, close proximity and orientations which deter intruders to the group, bodily contact and sharing speaking time all characterize a work group in which everybody gets on well.

Groups in which the pattern of interaction is like the second example will tend to be more effective than those in which it is like the first. It does not always follow, of course, that a happy group is a productive group. It may simply be a happy group. But, perhaps fortunately, it tends to be the case. Work would be a wretched affair indeed if the most effective groups were the most miserable ones.

The BL of industrial relations

In the context of British industrial relations, BL often stood for British Leyland and became associated in the popular mind with poor industrial relations and breakdowns in communication. Here, however, BL simply stands for body language. It has a greater bearing upon the relationships between management and workers than many people may be prepared to admit.

Since good industrial relations depend upon successful negotiations, fruitful meetings and give and take on both sides, the kind of body language which will be helpful will include increased eye contact, because this will help people to like each other better (or at least dislike each other a little less). Friendly facial expressions and smiles should help, though head nods and head cocks when listening may be less likely to be regarded as insincere. Gestures need to be rather limited, though there is a role for less inhibition when expressing emotions with which everybody present can be expected to agree. Forward lean in posture, with some asymmetry to make the situation less formal, will help, as will, for the same reason, rather closer proximity, modified perhaps with indirect orientation. Bodily contact appropriate to industrial relations probably extends no further than the handshake when agreement has been reached and, in greetings and farewells, the occasional slap on the back and the reassuring hand on the back of the upper arm.

Motivating others

Body language to motivate will include, again, increased eye contact, positive facial expressions, head nods and head cocks when listening to others' problems or point of view on work-related matters. Open gestures, forward postures, closer proximity, direct orientation, appropriate bodily contact and supportive vocalizations will all help to create the kind of climate in which people are likely to feel motivated. Appearance is probably a minor matter here, but timing and synchronization can become very important. If people are to feel motivated, they must feel that they can contribute to discussions and meetings. If they have difficulty in achieving this, something has to be done to assist them.

Team building

Warren Lamb took the view that it is impossible to separate postures and gestures: they merge together in such a way that you have to consider both simultaneously. He also believed that if people are to be welded together into effective teams, it helps considerably if their posture-gesture merging patterns match each other, or are at least complementary.

There is no doubt that patterns of non-verbal communication do affect how well a number of people develop into a team, but we really need to consider the influence of all aspects of body language rather than just two of them.

One of the most noticeable characteristics of many effective teams is that many of the members look alike. We tend to feel we can work better, and even generally interact more comfortably, with people who are similar in appearance to ourselves. There is more than a grain of truth in the old adage 'Birds of a feather flock together'. There will also be similarities in the use of all the other aspects of body language.

Sometimes, there may not be similarity so much as complementarity – that is, a dominant person and a submissive person will often get along very well together because their body language dovetails. Dominant people like to control and regulate interaction, submissive people will happily allow this and may actually welcome it because it removes the necessity for them to make active decisions when they would far rather be passive.

EXERCISES AND EXPERIMENTS

1 What's my line?

If you can enlist the participation of a few other people, get them to take it in turns to portray an occupation by using body language alone. The others have to guess what the occupation is. Which kinds of job are easiest to portray non-verbally? Which are the easiest to guess? Are both categories made up of the same jobs?

2 The ideal workmate

Make a list of the non-verbal behaviours you would look for in an ideal workmate. Use the headings eye contact, facial expressions, head movements, gestures, postures, proximity and orientation, bodily contact, appearance and physique, timing and synchronization, and non-verbal aspects of speech.

3 Guess who's coming to work

Imagine that a new worker at your own place of work was as opposite in appearance to you and your workmates as possible (for instance, if you are all middle-aged and White, that he or she is young and Black). How would this affect the way in which the group or team you work with operates?

4 Haway the lads!

Study the members of your local football team and the way they play. Is the use of body language a factor which affects how well they play? Which players seem to operate best together? Is this purely because of footballing skill or does body language affect the situation?

13 | EVERYDAY ENCOUNTERS

In addition to work, there are all kinds of other places in which we meet people and all kinds of people that we meet. These encounters can range from the briefest passing and acknowledgement of someone in the street to an extremely formal and prolonged evening function at which we have to be on our best behaviour, conversing and acting according to quite rigid rules, perhaps for several hours.

Consider the day of a fairly typical family. Mother gets up and the first people she meets are her husband and children. If she is a housewife, she could during the day meet neighbours, friends, the postman, the meter reader for the gas or electricity board, the person delivering mail orders, shopkeepers, other customers, other mothers meeting their children from school, the babysitter, members of the parent–teachers' committee, and people in the pub after the meeting. Father meets his wife and children, and then possibly the newsagent, the station ticket inspector, fellow passengers, fellow office workers, restaurant staff, friends in the pub after work, and people in the pub when he finally catches up with his wife. The children meet their parents, friends, classmates, teachers, shopkeepers, members of a children's theatre group touring schools, and the babysitter.

In each of these encounters, our own body language and that of other people will be continuously supporting (or contradicting), regulating or controlling the interaction which takes place. It forms a constant stream of activity throughout every waking hour. It is particularly important at the beginnings of encounters, and how we behave then can more or less determine the eventual outcome of the entire meeting.

EXERCISE: AGE AND SEX

Tape record the voices of several people of various ages. Record males and females in roughly equal proportions. Have them talk about subjects which will not give their age away (for example, avoid having an older man talking about his war stories). Play the tapes to other people and see if they can identify the age and sex of the speakers from voice alone.

If you are unable to enlist the participation of other people, sit with your back to the television and see if you can guess the age and sex of several speakers. Note these down in your notebook. Then watch the picture as well as listening to the sound and see if this helps you to decide how accurate you were. If you can find out from a *Who's Who*-type reference book of television personalities how old people actually are, so much the better.

Exercise review

As you might expect, it is not too difficult in most cases to identify a person's sex from voice alone. It is often also quite easy, incidentally, to identify race or nationality. You will probably have found, whichever form of the experiment you tried, that children's voices can be spotted without difficulty. Very old people often have a voice quality that is relatively easy to distinguish. The real problem comes with people whose ages are approximately between thirty and seventy.

There are some clues which can be used. Volume tends to be higher with younger people than with older ones. Tone tends to deepen with age, though it tends to sharpen and sound quite fragile with extreme age, and may develop a tremor. Younger voices have a more confident, even brash, sound to them in many cases. If more than two-thirds of the voices were correctly allocated to age and sex, this would be a good result (allow five years either side for age).

The first five minutes

In the first five minutes of an encounter, particularly an encounter with a stranger, we are heavily dependent upon body language for information about the other person; what he or she is like, how easy or difficult they are going to be to deal with, whether we are going to like them, and so on. We depend on body language because the opening stages of conversations tend to centre around small talk and general trivia, like the weather, and we do not begin to get detailed verbal information until later. It is interesting to note that we do not seem to be prepared to defer our judgements until we have this information. We seem to need to have to size people up quickly. Hence the dependence on body language.

These first impressions tend to last. The fact that they are formed very quickly does not seem to detract from their strength and permanence. Indeed, they can even be affected by what we are told about someone in advance of meeting them. If we are told that we will like someone because they are friendly, we can be conditioned by this and respond in a friendly manner when we do meet them.

We assess people on several counts when we first meet them. We rate their attractiveness, which does not merely mean rating their sexual attraction to us. For most people, however, if the person is an attractive member of the opposite sex, this will be a factor. We will return to personal attraction in the next chapter, because it does have a strong influence upon us in our society and depends almost entirely on body language for its effect.

As a part of attraction assessment, we determine the other's sex. If this is difficult, as it may be with some women with deep voices, very small breasts and a male body shape, or with some men who are soft-skinned and have female gestures and postures, the resulting confusion can adversely affect the communication between us. Although all men and women are equal, we do respond differently to persons of the opposite sex. These differences might disappear as society becomes more sexually egalitarian, but they are still with us and cannot be ignored.

We try to assess a person's age. Again, our responses to people we perceive as being older than ourselves will differ from those we make to younger people. These responses will also be affected by our perceptions of the other's status. We respond differently if a younger person is of high status or an older person is of low status. Things may change if we become more socially egalitarian, but here, too, we have a long way to go.

Other aspects of people which we assess in the first few minutes include their voice quality, their race or nationality, general appearance and physique, likely occupation, where they live, and their educational and cultural background. We may also assess their social and political attitudes and opinions from their use of body language.

Opening and closing conversations

At the beginning of an encounter the kinds of body language which can be observed include a great deal of eye contact, as we are forming the first impressions we have just discussed, and facial expressions which are more likely to be positive, in the form of smiles, than negative. If they had been likely to be negative, we would have done whatever we could to avoid the encounter in the first place.

There will probably also have been eyebrow flash on first recognizing our companion, head cocks as we show interest in what news they have for us, forward lean, close proximity and direct orientation, handshakes and perhaps hugs or holding the upper arm with the free hand while shaking the hand with the other.

These behaviours are then followed in the initial stages of most conversations with stereotyped exchanges of the 'How are you?' 'I'm fine, how are you?' variety. The conversation will either shortly move on to more substantial matters or will tend to be short-lived. After the transition point, the body language settles down into the turn-taking in eye contact described in Chapter 1. Facial expressions and head movements will change to suit the verbal content of the conversation. Gestures will emphasize points being made, orientation may change so that it does not remain constantly direct and perhaps threatening. Both participants will unconsciously synchronize with each other, as described in Chapter 9. The encounter is well under way.

Mark Knapp and some of his colleagues investigated what they call 'the rhetoric of goodbye'. They identified a number of items of body language which seem to accompany the endings of conversations. These include breaking eye contact, left positioning (in which the person wishing to depart is pointing towards his or her proposed exit), forward lean, increased head nods, major movements of the legs, and smiling. Other behaviours which may be present include sweeping hand movements and, when sitting down, an uncrossing of the legs with a striking of the foot against the floor, using the hands to lever oneself out of the chair, perhaps preceded by striking the hands on the arms of the chair as if to say, 'Right, that's it, then, we've finished what we wanted to say to each other' – indeed, such verbalizations may actually accompany the body language.

How to spot a liar

There is an old joke about how to tell when a politician is lying, which runs as follows. When he smiles, he is telling the truth. When he points an accusing finger, he is telling the truth. But when he opens his mouth, he is lying. Clearly, in real life no such easy and simple criteria apply. But there are certain behaviours which occur more often when people are lying than when they are telling the truth.

Leakage (non-verbal behaviour which an individual fails to control and which can give clues as to the real truth) most frequently occurs, as we have seen, in the lower half of the body. Shuffling the feet, twitching the toes, crossing and uncrossing the legs, and so on, increase when we are trying to deceive others.

Attempts at deception do also involve the upper half of the body to some extent. Facial expressions may be capable of control, and an accomplished liar may be able to maintain eye contact with his listener, but the movements of the hands are less easily controllable. One gesture has been found to be common amongst those seeking to deceive. This is the hand shrug in which the hands are rotated so as to expose the palms. It is used to signal helplessness. It is as if deceivers were trying to enlist our sympathy because they could not help themselves.

Touching the side of the nose, touching the eye, licking the lips. drumming the fingers and gripping arm rests, whilst not in themselves being indicative solely of falsehood, do occur more often when people are attempting to deceive others. It comes down again to context. We have to keep reminding ourselves that there are very few pieces of body language which have meaning on their own regardless of context.

Albert Mehrabian, when he investigated how people behaved when they were conveying truthful messages and how they behaved when the messages were untruthful, discovered that those who were lying talked less, talked more slowly, and made more speech errors. Their rate of body movement also seemed to be slower.

Blushing, perspiration, voice tremors, gulping, shaking and playing with pencils or spectacles are other fairly obvious activities to watch for in people who are not telling the truth. Liars are less likely to engage in bodily contact or even to approach closely. Their body language very often contradicts their spoken words. For instance, they may say they would be very willing to submit themselves to a full enquiry and yet their facial expression may show distaste and their gestures and posture closed. Body language is nearly always a better guide to the truth than even the most eloquent words.

Small talk

Vague, inconsequential chats about another person's general (though not specific) health, the weather, the fortunes of the local football, rugby or cricket team and similar matters may seem to some people to be hardly worth spending time on. Yet they can have an importance quite out of proportion to their apparent significance.

During small talk, when the verbal content is – to say the least – undemanding, we can give most of our concentration to other people's body language– and we do. We can even, if we wish, systematically turn our attention to each aspect of body language so that we can learn more about the other person in less time than it would take to do so purely intuitively. Another advantage of a systematic approach is that it enables us to check that we have not missed an aspect out.

Next time you meet someone for a casual chat about nothing in particular or the next time you meet a stranger at a party, try the following approach. Take each aspect of body language discussed in this book in sequence and consider how the other is using it.

First, eye contact: do they use much or little? Do they appear to want more or less eye contact? How dilated are their pupils? Are they left breakers or right breakers? Do they keep looking around at other people, or is their full attention given to you?

Secondly, consider facial expressions. Are they positive or negative? Smiles and interest or scowls and disgust? Are there few or many changes in expression? Are there any micromomentary facial expressions you can spot?

What about head movements? Do they show interest with head cocks? Do they encourage you to speak with head nods? Do they respond to your head nods? Does the rhythm of their head movements fit the rhythm of their speech?

Next, are their gestures few or many? Are they expressive? Are they appropriate? Are they open or closed? Do they fold their arms in front of themselves or set up other barriers? If they cross their legs, which way do they cross them, towards you or away from you?

Look at the posture – is it upright or stooping? Do they use backward or forward lean?

Consider proximity and orientation. Do they approach closely or not? If you move closer, do they back away or turn to a less direct orientation? What do you do if they move closer? Is their orientation direct or indirect? Is it symmetrical or asymmetrical? Horizontal or vertical?

Now consider their use of bodily contact. Do they use any? In greetings only? Are they touchers or non-touchers? Which parts of the body do they touch most frequently as they are talking? Arms, hands, shoulders, backs or elsewhere? Does the touching, where it occurs, signal greater intimacy between you or only the other's wish for greater intimacy?

Next, assess their appearance and physique and how you feel it affects your response. Do you find them attractive? Are they taller than you or shorter? Does this have any affect? Are they fat or thin?

Does this affect your response to them?

What about their timing and synchronization? Does the discussion you are having dovetail neatly or do you find yourselves both speaking at the same time? If so, why? Nervousness or a failure to synchronize for some other reason?

Finally, listen to the non-verbal aspects of their speech. Do they make many speech errors? How fast do they speak? Do they speak loudly or softly? Have they a harsh tone or a smooth tone? How do the non-verbal aspects of their speech affect your response to them?

There are, of course, many other questions that can be posed, but these should provide you with a simple, yet systematic method of evaluating how other people use body language in everyday encounters. You should then be able to improve your use of body language without becoming too self-conscious and deliberate. Practice will, in any case, make things progressively easier and more natural.

EXERCISES AND EXPERIMENTS

1 Who said that?

Obtain photographs of several people, taken in what for them is a normal environment. Then get them to tape record a couple of minutes' speech about a topic which will not give the environment away. See if other people can match the voices to the photographs. How successful are they?

2 How many people do you meet a day?

Make a list of all the people you meet in a day. Be careful not to miss anyone out. Then classify them into friends, family, acquaintances, strangers and non-persons (people like waiters, bus drivers, canteen staff, and so on with whom the interaction is purely functional) What is the pattern of your daily interactions? Are you spending as much time with friends and family as you would like? If not, is there anything you can do about it?

3 What's the first thing you notice?

When you meet strangers, what is the first thing about them that you notice? Does it differ for males and females? For older people and for younger people? What are the physical characteristics you look for (or respond to) in an attractive stranger of the opposite sex?

4 Tell the truth

Either watch a television programme in which people claim to be telling the truth, and see how accurately you can identify the truth tellers – or get a group together to play the game. What deception cues help you to eliminate those least likely to be truthful? Ask those who seem to be able to pick out the right person more often than other people if they know how they do it. You will probably find that many of them put it down to a hunch and are totally unaware of how they have been influenced by body language.

14 | PERSONAL ATTRACTION

True though it may be that beauty is in the eye of the beholder, it is still possible to influence what the eye sees in the first place. Knowledge is always power and knowing more, as we now do, about what people find attractive enables us to take steps to present them with what they wish to see – or at least come closer to it than we might if we were in ignorance.

But why should we bother? One reason is that those who are perceived by others as being attractive are credited with having other attributes. Several studies have shown that they are more likely to be regarded as being talented, warm and responsive, kind, sensitive, interesting, poised, sociable and outgoing. When compared with unattractive people, they are seen as having a socially desirable personality, as having higher occupational status, as being more maritally competent, as more intelligent and as being happier. Whether all attractive people possess these qualities or not is clearly open to doubt. But if they are perceived as having them, this will tend to encourage their development anyway. Truth is not always reality, but what people perceive as reality. In other words, if they think it is true, then, for all practical purposes, it is true. As we said at the beginning, beauty is indeed in the eye of the beholder.

So what is it that we are looking for? Who and what do we find attractive? Most of the studies carried out seem to suggest that men look for those characteristics in women which differentiate them from men: fuller lips, narrower eyebrows, a softer complexion, absence of facial hair, large firm breasts, a narrower waist, relatively broad hips and long legs are all usually regarded as attractive. Glenn Wilson and David Nias describe a study which revealed that, over the years, Miss World has on average been an English-speaking model, aged 21, 5ft 8ins tall, blonde with brown eyes and with vital statistics of 35–24–35. Clearly, many women who do not match these stereotypes are regarded by men as attractive – nevertheless, studies which ask people to rate photographs of attractive women find that most respondents will agree on who they find the most attractive. But averages always do, after all, conceal a range of individual variations.

It is not quite as easy to identify what it is that women find attractive in men. Men imagine that they look for tallness, a muscular chest and shoulders, muscular biceps and a large penis. At least one study found, however, that women were more interested in a man's eyes, whether or not he was slim and whether he had small and sexy buttocks. A number of studies have found that women are much more interested in a man's personality, dependability and general character.

Mark Cook and Robert McHenry quote a study which suggested that the ideal face for both sexes is oval in shape with a clear complexion, large blue eyes, a straight nose, a medium-sized mouth, ears which do not protrude, long eyelashes, bushy eyebrows for men and fine eyebrows for women. No face, however, is perfectly symmetrical, so some variation from the ideal is inevitable.

In reality, personal attraction does not depend simply on appearance and physique. Every aspect of body language has a contribution to make and we often overlook a less-than-perfect face or figure when, say, pupil dilation is high with plenty of eye contact, facial expressions and gestures are expressive, or we like the sound of someone's voice.

EXERCISE: TEN OUT OF TEN

Some readers will remember the film *10*, starring Bo Derek and Dudley Moore, based in part on the idea of scoring the attractiveness of people on a scale running from one to ten. The film was based on a long-standing habit of young Western males when looking for the company of young, attractive females. This exercise seeks to apply the same approach to persons of either sex.

Using the rating scale in Figure 14.1 (make as many copies of it as you need), rate several strangers over the next week. If you can, enlist the participation of others so that you finish up with a reasonably large number of completed scales.

Score people 1 to 10 on each of the following aspects of appearance and other uses of body language. Place a X in the appropriate box.

	1	2	3	4	5	6	7	8	9	10
Hair										
Forehead										
Shape of head										
Face										
Eyes										
Nose										
Mouth										
Ears										
Neck										
Skin										
Body build										
Shoulders										
Chest/breasts										
Arms										
Hands										
Waist										
Buttocks										
Abdomen and pelvis										
Thighs										
Knees										
Calves										
Feet										
Shape of legs										
Length of legs										
Eye contact										
Facial expression										
Head movements										
Gestures										
Posture and stance										
Proximity and orientation										
Bodily contact										
Timing and synchronization										
Non-verbal aspects of speech										
TOTALS:										

(For a 0 rating simply
leave blank)
Max = 330

Figure 14.1 Personal Attraction Assessment Scale

Exercise review

Two things should emerge from this exercise. You should obtain a clearer idea of precisely which non-verbal behaviours and physical characteristics appeal to you in other people. You should also find that your ratings tend to agree with those of others who took part in the experiment (if you were fortunate enough to find some friends or colleagues who would).

Which is more important, appearance or some other aspect of body language?

Boy meets girl

Let us visualize a first encounter between a young man and a young woman in a pub, disco or night club and see what body language they might use to initiate interaction and begin to get to know each other. We shall call the young man Pete.

Pete enters and pauses just inside the door, looking around. His thumbs are hitched into the waist of his jeans and his hands are hanging loose. Even so they seem to be pointing towards his crotch, though not in an obvious way. Without realizing it, he is already indicating to all the unattached women present that he is looking for a partner. If his stance is too overtly sexual, he will be seen as regarding himself as 'God's gift to women'. Pete is already in danger of coming on too strong and turning the women off. As his eyes become accustomed to the rather subdued lighting, he spies an empty table and makes for it. He sits down, crosses one leg loosely over the other so that an ankle rests on a knee, orders a drink from the attractive floor waitress and continues looking around. He doesn't realize it yet, but he is already being watched himself and every move he makes is telling the watcher something about him.

At a table beside the small area set aside for dancing, a group of young women is sitting chatting. They appear to be wrapped up in each other's conversation, but in reality they are barely listening to each other. As they talk, glances dart towards the boys around the room. They are picking out the ones they will respond to if asked to dance. One of them, Susie, a pert, fashionably-dressed eighteen-year-old with short, dark hair, is already interested in Pete and keeps glancing in his direction. Pete catches one of these glances and continues looking at her after she has looked away He likes what he sees, but what should he do?

Once he is aware that Susie keeps looking at him, he contrives to return the look with increasing frequency. The moment comes when their eyes are almost locked together. He wants to look away, as does Susie, and if the mutual gaze continues too long without a development one of them will have to break gaze and look away. This will cause the one who does so some embarrassment and may therefore set in train a negative reaction, which will make subsequent communication more difficult. Before that can happen, he smiles. A slight, warm, friendly smile. Susie smiles back. He nods barely perceptibly towards the dance floor. Susie nods agreement, blushing slightly even though she doesn't really feel embarrassed, just a tingling sensation of pleasurable anticipation. He gets up, goes over, asks her to dance and they go on to the floor. With hardly a word before success was assured, he has surmounted the biggest barrier in human communication, the invitation to interact in the initial encounter. But he is not yet home and dry by any means and there are numerous pitfalls still to avoid.

Because the lights are low and the music is on the loud side, Pete and Susie will not have much opportunity to talk. If his initial attraction to her (and hers toward him) is maintained once they are close enough to find out if the other is taller or shorter than desired, or fatter or thinner, or has undesirable breath or body odour, or is as physically attractive as seemed to be the case at some distance, or has an unacceptable accent or voice quality, then they will both be sizing each other up on a number of characteristics.

They will assess each other (as we saw in Chapter 13) without knowing it, on whether the other gives the amount and kind of eye contact desired (if he now keeps glancing too obviously at other women it will tend to put Susie off), on facial expression (if he doesn't smile again she may interpret it as loss of interest), body posture and orientation (if he keeps dancing with his back to her, she will go and sit down with her friends), gestures (if she keeps stroking her hair, he may see her as vain), and a host of other non-verbal behaviours. If they go on liking what they see, the moment will come when Susie will abandon her friends and sit with Pete between dancing periods. He will be over the second hurdle. Their relationship will have progressed a stage.

How will Pete know that Susie likes him and is not just passing the time until something better walks in the door? What signals will she give? Nothing can be completely certain because, as we now know, non-verbal communication is more dependent on context than verbal communication.

If he looks into her eyes, he may notice that the pupils are dilated. If his general assessment of her indicates that she is neither drugged nor drunk, he may interpret this as a sign of interest.

She might not actually blush, but her facial colouring may be heightened. This can be a favourable sign, as can perspiration, however slight (as long as it's not simply the result of dancing or because the place is over-warm). Although she might not stroke her hair vainly all the time, occasional grooming gestures and clothes-straightening (especially pulling down a sweater slightly so that it emphasizes the breasts) can be signals of interest and even readiness for sexual activity.

We can now leave Pete and Susie to enjoy themselves and each other, secure in the knowledge that, even though they have not yet had the opportunity to talk to each other in detail (the music is still too loud for this), their bodies have already spoken volumes.

Take your partners

The example of Pete and Susie illustrates some of the general principles of using body language to find attractive mates and even to establish relationships of a less permanent nature. In many ways, these are similar to those which are important in establishing friendships generally.

Eye contact between lovers and friends has an even greater importance than it has, as we saw, at work and in everyday encounters. As greater looking often leads to greater liking, the duration of mutual gaze will be extended.

Facial expressions will tend to be positive, if only because one is in the presence of people one feels close to. But it is also true that, simply because of this, negative expressions will be more readily tolerated. What are friends and lovers for, after all, if you cannot simply relax and show them how you are really feeling?

Similarly, it is not necessary to attend to head movements, gestures and posture. Proximity and orientation, however, do need more attention. Close friends and lovers will suspect something is amiss if greater proximity is not permitted. Something similar will apply if the orientation is not reasonably direct. Bodily contact will also be more frequent and, in the case of lovers, if this is not frequent and extensive, it will be inferred that all is not as well as it should be.

Appearance may not seem to matter much, but it does. If you persist in dressing totally differently, having a different hairstyle or making-up (or not making-up) in an odd way, at the very least this will provoke leg-pulling comments and at the worst it will lead to your exclusion from the group.

Timing and synchronization may tend to look after themselves, but the non-verbal aspects of speech will be important. If your accent does not fit in, or your voice is too loud and your friends are quiet, or your tone is harsh and your friends are gentle people, you could well have problems.

Careful attention to the key areas of body language between lovers and friends will not be misplaced. You may find that some study of the body language of those closest to you will provide insights into the key areas in the specific context in which you find yourself.

Getting on with people

Empathy is the term often used to describe the ability to be able to view a situation or problem from someone else's point of view. Successful empathy, of the kind necessary in counselling, depends on a more than usually sensitive response to the body language of others and on using it more effectively oneself. Essentially, empathy is a question of adjusting to what other parties to the interaction feel is appropriate.

If they want more eye contact, greater proximity, direct orientation or bodily contact, you can provide it. With facial expression or gestures, because the other might make no obvious indication as to preference, you will need to use all your sensitivity in deciding what is appropriate. You can let them give the lead in timing and synchronization, appearance and non-verbal aspects of speech.

As far as head nods are concerned, the initiative lies with you. Since their role is to draw out, to reinforce and to reassure, a liberal use of head nods (single and double of normal size – not exaggerated) will help to encourage the verbal flow necessary for effective counselling. As counselling and advising are everyday skills as well as professional skills, these approaches have a far-reaching significance.

Star quality

Stars possess charisma. That is what makes them stars and makes them stand out from the crowd. But how do charismatic personalities use body language? Is their use of it what makes them stars? If it is, can the rest of us learn how to become stars?

Certainly, body language must be an important factor. Our everyday experience tells us that there are many good singers, good actors, good dancers, and good comedians, but only a few of them become stars. Clearly, luck plays a part – you have to be in the right place at the right time. But body language is also crucial.

Charisma is difficult to define, but it seems to be a quality that some people have which draws others' eyes to them, which makes people defer to them and which causes them to be raised on to a pedestal in the popular mind. It is most common in leaders (whether political or otherwise), entertainers and sports personalities. But it is present to some degree in many of the people you meet in the course of an average day. The old man in the pub who is a 'bit of a character' has charisma. So does the captain of the school soccer team whom the girls have a crush on. So does the guard on the train who chats to her passengers over the public address system and at the end of the journey commends them to the safe-keeping of the Almighty.

As far as their use of body language is concerned, charismatic individuals will be dominant rather than submissive. Stars (even the stars of everyday life) will be high on gaze and mutual gaze, or eye contact. For some stars it is the most important aspect of body language. They love to look and, especially, to be looked at. They blossom in the limelight of others' attention. They feed upon it and thrive upon it. They look around at their audiences. They use anticipatory scanning when moving through a crowd of fans.

Stars smile and grin a great deal Their facial expressions are always fast-changing and expressive. Either that or, perhaps in the case of some pop singers, they are sullen, with lowered brows and a seductive expression.

A common head movement with stars is to toss the head backwards. It often occurs at pauses in songs or when taking the audience's applause. If they have long hair, it is quite a dramatic gesture. In the case of teenage idols, it can on its own provoke squeals of delight from the fans, as can many other body movements. The head is often tilted back, as if to allow everyone as clear a view of it as possible.

Gestures are important to a star. They must be open and the hands are frequently palm up with the arms stretching out as if to embrace the audience. Palm-up or palm-outwards gestures of various kinds and an avoidance of closed, defensive gestures help, as it were, to bring the audience into the interaction: their role as receivers might make them passive and therefore less likely to applaud unless they were brought in in this way. Gestures are often self-manipulative – stroking the hair, picking pieces of fluff off the clothing, straightening clothes – and may even be overtly sexual in nature.

Posture tends to be upright with some forward lean. Very often one arm is extended with the hand palm up and the other hand is on the hip. Proximity is not usually close, except when moving through fans, though television close-ups can give the illusion of proximity. Orientation towards the audience will usually be direct and stems from an old convention in the theatre that, as in teaching, you never turn your back on your audience. Orientation in situations like television chat shows may be asymmetrical and indirect as there is usually an attempt to create a relaxing and informal atmosphere in which interviewees will disclose more about themselves than they might otherwise.

Bodily contact is infrequent. Stars are nearly always people you look at but do not touch This may be part of the reason why pop fans will often go to great lengths to get close enough to touch their idols.

Appearance is almost always highly attractive or highly unusual. If stars looked like chartered accountants or shop assistants, it would be more difficult for us to put them on their pedestals. For this kind of reason, they are often more heavily made up and their style of dress is both colourful and fashionable.

Their timing and synchronization are sharp and dominant. They talk a lot and often in a fast, breathy, 'mid-Atlantic' accent. They especially like to talk about themselves and their successes.

This may seem to provide a stereotypical picture of a star, which is unfortunate – stars are, by definition, individuals. There have to be things about them which distinguish them from others. That must be remembered. All we can do here is highlight some of the aspects of body language which accompany star quality. You do not have to practise them all before you can become a star.

How to be more attractive

Of all the aspects of body language that have been discussed, which are the ones that will make other people think you more attractive? Let us take each aspect in turn and see what we should be doing:

1 *Eye contact*: Lookers are normally preferred to non-lookers. Give people as much eye contact as you think they can take.

2 *Facial expressions*: Be lively. Smile a lot in a warm, friendly manner. Let your face register interest.

3 *Head movements*: Use single and double head nods to encourage others to speak and to show attention on your part. Use head cocks for the same reasons. Keep your chin up, literally.

4 *Gestures*: Be expressive, without overdoing it. Perhaps the best way is to keep your hands out of your pockets and avoid arm-folding and other barrier gestures. Use open gestures.

5 *Posture*: When standing, be reasonably erect. When seated, adopt backward leaning asymmetrical posture for informality. Adopt forward leaning, symmetrical posture for showing interest. Use open postures.

6 *Proximity and orientation*: Approach as closely as you can without embarrassing others. Use a 0° orientation wherever possible.

7 *Bodily contact*: Touch as often as you can without causing offence. Encourage touching from others.

8 *Appearance and physique*: Dress according to group norms, but go for colour where you can. Keep skin soft and smooth. Keep slim. This applies to both sexes, but men may have to restrict colour a little more and do not need to have such soft skins.

9 *Timing and synchronization*: Be sensitive to the operation of these factors, as discussed in Chapter 9.

10 *Non-verbal aspects of speech*: Do not talk too much or too fast, but try to talk as well as listen in roughly equal proportions. People like listeners, but attractive people talk more. You will have to balance the two. Control volume, pitch and tone to suit the environment. Aim for a reasonably standard accent and avoid regional extremes.

If you feel you are presently deficient in your body language in more than two of these areas, you should be able to improve your attractiveness to others significantly and noticeably.

EXERCISES AND EXPERIMENTS

1 Who makes the first move?

Observe people in a place where they are meeting for the first time (a party or a dance, say). Who initiates interaction? The male, who, in Western culture, still tends to adopt an outgoing role? Or the female, perhaps by permitting longer than normal eye contact? What body language brings two male or two female strangers together (except in homosexual encounters)? How does this differ from a mixed-sex encounter?

2 Stargazing

Study television stars. How do they use the ten aspects of body language we have discussed in this chapter? What differences do you notice from what has been suggested here? Try to meet some stars in person and conduct the same analysis. Are there any differences between their behaviour in real life and their behaviour on television?

3 Partners for life

Study the body language of people you know who have been happily married for at least ten years. Do they echo each others' postures and gestures? Do they echo any other aspects of body language? How does their behaviour differ when they are apart from when they are together?

4 Hello, sexy

What are the body language components of sex appeal? List them under the ten headings used in this chapter. If you can, compare your assessment with those of several other people. On which aspects do you agree?

15 | **PERSONAL DEVELOPMENT**

There is clearly some value in developing body language skills for their own sakes, as there is in developing any other personal skill. But the value is enhanced if the aim is greater effectiveness in communication and improvement is seen as making a contribution to personal growth and the exploitation of human potential.

Body language is so central to self-presentation and impression management that it makes good sense to see its development as but a means to an end. If, in presenting ourselves to the world at large and seeking to manage or control the impression we make upon it, we can achieve this larger purpose of personal development, then the work done in the course of using this book will have acquired additional usefulness.

By now it should be clear that, as we claimed in the Introduction, body language can be improved – and by now, if you have been carrying out the exercises and experiments at the end of each chapter, you should see in yourself signs of that improvement. But we might be able to take things further, and it will be the task of this chapter to show how the work done so far can be continued after you have finished the book and how you can continue using body language to increasingly better effect. It would, after all, be less than fully useful if, at the end of the book, you closed it and said to yourself, 'Right, that's it. I've done body language, what's next?' Clearly, whatever improvements had been made would soon disappear. There have to be continuation and follow-up if improvements are to be maintained and consolidated to provide a solid base for even further improvements.

EXERCISE: SECRET MESSAGES

There are many non-verbal games that you can play, if you can enlist the cooperation of family or friends, which will help to develop your use of body language in a general way and thus contribute to your personal development. We shall look at some of them in this chapter, here and at the end, and you should try to find opportunities to play as many of them as possible. If you are using this book as a class text, your tutor should be able to arrange for the games to be played in the classroom. This first game involves the non-verbal transmission of messages.

Write numbers on pieces of paper sufficient for the number of players (for instance, if there are five players, use the numbers 1 to 5). Give all the pieces of paper to one person. Everyone sits in a circle around this person, who gives each of the other players a numbered piece of paper which they keep concealed from the others. The person in the middle calls out two numbers (say, 2 and 5). The players with these numbers have to change places. The person in the middle has to try to take one of their places. Since no one knows anyone else's number, the players must first find out non-verbally which players have the numbers called. They must make sure the person in the middle does not also find out. If the person in the middle succeeds in taking a player's place when the changeover occurs then that player goes into the middle, everyone gives him or her the numbered pieces of paper, which he or she shuffles and redistributes. The game then begins again. It can be played until everyone has had a turn in the middle or until everyone is tired of it. No one may speak, except the person in the middle calling the numbers.

Exercise review

In playing this game, there are certain things worth looking out for. How, for instance, do the players establish who the numbered players are without the person in the middle finding out? Which aspects of body language do they use? How can the person in the middle best catch the non-verbal messages which pass between players? Is it more difficult to make others understand your number or to understand someone else's? How do players signal the moment when they wish to change places?

Sometimes a kind of conspiracy against the person in the middle can develop in which several players pretend to be the nominated numbers. This produces confusion and makes it easier for players to change places. You will find it useful to make a list of the things you learn from playing this and the other games in this chapter.

Establishing rapport

For successful communication to take place between you and other people, and for you to find that each encounter makes some small contribution to furthering personal development, you need to become skilled in establishing rapport with others. For this to happen with relative ease you need clear channels of communication, some degree of trust in, and acceptance of, the other person and a smooth pattern of interaction.

There are several things you can do to create rapport. You can use a warm, friendly manner, together with smiles and eye contact at appropriate points in the interaction. You can make rapport more likely by treating the other person as an equal. You can establish the smooth and easy pattern of interaction that is needed by using the various techniques discussed in this book.

Finding a common interest or experience can help to create a bond between people, which makes it easier to establish rapport. Showing a keen, sympathetic interest in the other person, giving them your full attention, making it clear that there is plenty of time for the encounter, and listening carefully to what they say will all help. You can adopt the other's terminology and conventions, and generally meet them on their own ground.

In discussion, you will need to keep the other person involved in the interaction. You will need to motivate them and make them want to take part. You will need to reduce any anxiety or defensiveness shown by the other and you should be concerned to see that the impression you make on the other is a good one.

Clearly, many of these things can be achieved by using appropriate body language. Eye contact will be higher than average. Facial expressions will show interest and a good deal of use will be made of smiles. Head movements will, in the main, consist of nods and head cocks. Gestures will be open and encouraging. Postures will be forward more often than not. Proximity will be close and orientation either direct or side by side. Bodily contact will often be appropriate, holding a hand or placing an arm round a shoulder.

Rapport is easier to establish between people who look and dress alike, so this aspect of body language may be important. Timing and synchronization will be crucial and it is better if you let the other person dictate the pace and style of interaction and seek to fit in with it and encourage it. This can be helped by using non-verbal aspects of speech, such as a soft tone, low volume and various supportive vocalizations.

Self-disclosure

Sidney Jourard has done a great deal of research into what he calls 'the transparent self', or the willingness of people to disclose information about themselves to others. He has shown that people will disclose more and behave differently when the person they are with has first let him- or herself be known in various respects. In other words, if you wish to find out more about a person you are more likely to achieve this if you first volunteer information about yourself. This can be done both verbally and non-verbally.

Non-verbally, you can engage in self-disclosure by, for instance, using a greater variety of facial expressions, by an increased use of gestures and by more changes in posture. All bodily movement makes a contribution to enabling others to make an assessment of us.

It is often easier to disclose yourself to a stranger than to a friend. If people think they are unlikely to see someone again, that person acquires 'stranger value' and more is disclosed, especially of inner thoughts and feelings.

Self-disclosure is worth encouraging, both in yourself and in others. It leads to self-awareness and knowledge and these in turn lead to self-development and personal growth.

Interactive skills

It would be remiss of us if we were to complete our consideration of how to use body language more effectively without giving some thought as to how non-verbal skills relate to other interactive skills. As we have seen, in any face-to-face encounter between people, a substantial part of what happens is non-verbal rather than verbal. Since, at the moment, a great deal of interactive skills training neglects or even totally ignores body language, there is a need to redress the balance.

An integrated approach to the development of interactive or social skills would contain several elements. There would be practice. Exercises and experiments like the ones in this book provide this. If responses are recorded, this makes it possible for you to provide yourself with feedback, which promotes further improvement.

Role-playing provides an excellent opportunity to integrate both verbal and non-verbal skills. In this kind of activity role-reversal, in which you assume a role opposite to that which you would normally occupy in a situation, is particularly useful. Examples might be fathers behaving as children, managers behaving as shop stewards, salesmen behaving as customers, and vice versa. Again, feedback (perhaps through the use of video taping) enables participants to judge how well or how badly they have performed. Games, of the kind suggested in this chapter, also help.

Imitations of models of good practice, discussions of situations with others and reading (perhaps of some of the books listed in the Further Reading section) will all make a contribution. Although caution has been urged over encounter groups, some people can find them useful. There are, however, alternative forms of sensitivity training which are less stressful. These include watching films or television programmes and then discussing people's behaviour with others; having someone read a passage and assessing the emotional state being portrayed when the words cannot be heard; or doing some elementary recording of body language in the way suggested later in this chapter.

If the involvement of others can be secured, so much the better, but you can still achieve a great deal on your own. The important point to keep in mind is that skill in using body language needs to be seen in the context of developing interactive skills generally.

Synergy

Synergy is said to occur when the outcome of a situation is greater than the sum of the inputs. It is sometimes described by the formula $2 + 2 = 5$. Examples of synergy might include the performance of a play that is not just good but gets several curtain calls from a rapturous audience; the football team which does not merely win its matches but seems as if it cannot lose; the party at which everybody really enjoys themselves and seems to go with that extra swing.

Non-verbally, synergy is promoted especially by sensitive timing and synchronization. When things are going so well and with such a rhythm that an occasion acquires a dimension of magic and a sense of being special, that is synergy. When everybody is working together so well that it seems as if they simply could not make a mistake, that is synergy. When an artist gives such a perfectly timed and paced performance that it is absolutely flawless, that is synergy.

Synergy can also be promoted by eye contact, head movement, gestures, postures and non-verbal aspects of speech where these have an influence on people's reactions to what has just happened and anticipation of what is about to happen. Things need to work together particularly well for synergy to be produced. When it is, it adds an extra quality which is well worth striving for.

Recording body language

For those who wish to pursue their study of body language further, it will be useful to make some more systematic recordings of non-verbal behaviour. Two possibilities follow.

■ First, while watching a chosen subject on television or in real life, record their body language on a coding sheet (see Figure 15.1). This can later be analyzed for the purpose of establishing patterns and to identify peculiarities in behavioural styles.

■ Second, record your responses to your subject's body
language on a rating scale (see Figure 15.2). This
should provide even more information for analysis and
assessment.

		e.g.	1	2	3	4	5	6	7	8	9
1	Eye contact	✓									
2	Facial expression change										
3	Head movement	✓									
4	Gestures	✓									
5	Posture change										
6	Proximity and orientation change										
7	Bodily contact										
8	Appearance (rate on scale 1 to 10)	8									
9	Timing and sychronization	✓									
10	Non-verbal aspects of speech	✓									
✓ if behaviour present											

10-second intervals

Figure 15.1 Body language coding sheet

EXERCISES AND EXPERIMENTS

1 Random groups

A group of players moves freely around a room. A person appointed
as the game leader calls out a number, such as two or four, and the
players have to form into groups of that size. No-one may speak.
Anyone left over drops out of the game. The game continues until
only two people remain. In this game, it is interesting to see who are
the most successful players and who are the least successful.
Differences in their use of body language should be detected.

2 Is a wink as good as a nod?

A group of players is divided into two groups. Half sit on chairs and
half stand behind the chairs, arranged in a circle. One chair is left
empty (i.e. there must be an odd number of players). The person
behind the empty chair has to wink at a seated player. That player
has to try to get to the empty chair and the person standing behind
has to try to prevent him or her. If he or she succeeds in preventing

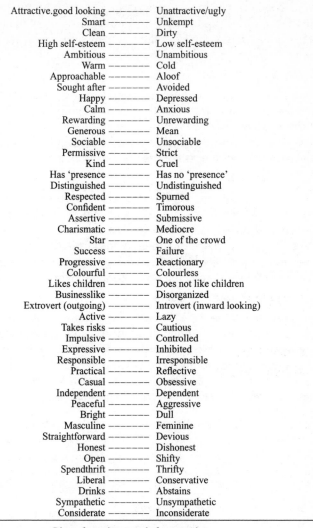

Attractive.good looking	Unattractive/ugly
Smart	Unkempt
Clean	Dirty
High self-esteem	Low self-esteem
Ambitious	Unambitious
Warm	Cold
Approachable	Aloof
Sought after	Avoided
Happy	Depressed
Calm	Anxious
Rewarding	Unrewarding
Generous	Mean
Sociable	Unsociable
Permissive	Strict
Kind	Cruel
Has 'presence'	Has no 'presence'
Distinguished	Undistinguished
Respected	Spurned
Confident	Timorous
Assertive	Submissive
Charismatic	Mediocre
Star	One of the crowd
Success	Failure
Progressive	Reactionary
Colourful	Colourless
Likes children	Does not like children
Businesslike	Disorganized
Extrovert (outgoing)	Introvert (inward looking)
Active	Lazy
Takes risks	Cautious
Impulsive	Controlled
Expressive	Inhibited
Responsible	Irresponsible
Practical	Reflective
Casual	Obsessive
Independent	Dependent
Peaceful	Aggressive
Bright	Dull
Masculine	Feminine
Straightforward	Devious
Honest	Dishonest
Open	Shifty
Spendthrift	Thrifty
Liberal	Conservative
Drinks	Abstains
Sympathetic	Unsympathetic
Considerate	Inconsiderate

Place ✓ at point on scale for example:

Clean ✓ Dirty

Warm ✓ Cold

Figure 15.2 Semantic differential rating scale for perceptions of others' non-verbal behaviour

the escape, both players change places and the person with the empty chair tries again. It is worth noticing if one attractive member of the group gets more winks than anyone else, and if seated players try to avoid being winked at by unattractive standing players.

3 The magic mirror

Each player finds a partner and stands facing them. The players try to move in such a way that they copy each other, as if they were mirror images. Those who observe the game should look to see who gives a lead, which people are better at copying than others and which people do things that are almost impossible to copy.

4 Silent drawing

A number of people sit round a piece of paper, supplied with crayons or felt-tipped pens of different colours. No one speaks. Each person contributes as much or as little as he or she wishes to create a drawing on the piece of paper. Who starts? Who does most? Who does nothing at all? How does the group decide it has finished? What are the most common non-verbal behaviours?

5 Come in if you can get in

The players wait outside a room. They come in one at a time and take up a position they find comfortable near people they like. No one may speak. The game finishes when everyone is finally placed. How many groups form? Who is left out? What body language do people use to show that they want someone to join them? How do they show they do not want someone to join them?

CONCLUSION

We are approaching the end of our consideration of body language, its nature, its uses and how it can be improved. You should not think of this as the end of your study of body language, however. You can continue that for the rest of your life, if you wish, by always paying more attention to non-verbal aspects of communication than you did before you read this book. Hopefully, you will have overcome the embarrassment that many people feel over discussion of body language. You should be able to regard it as a skill in the same way that reading, writing, listening and speaking are skills. As these can be improved by training, so can body language.

Of all the points that have been made in this book and of all the information which has been given, which are the most important? What are the essential features of body language that you should concentrate on and seek to develop in your everyday encounters with other people at work and at play? You are free, of course, to form your own opinions on this on the basis of what you have learned both from reading the book and from carrying out the exercises and experiments. You might nevertheless find it useful to have a view against which you can measure your own. Let us consider each aspect of body language separately, but remember that its effective use requires all aspects to be integrated. We must remind ourselves that we only separate the aspects for convenience of examination.

Eye contact should be encouraged. Avoid staring, but more eye contact is likely to lead to greater liking, greater awareness and more accurate understanding of others' body language. We have to remember that communication is as much a question of accurate reception of signals as it is of skilful transmission. Pupil size is a useful indicator of liking, at close quarters. As it is beyond conscious control, it can be more revealing than many other aspects of body language.

Facial expressions should be lively and expressive rather than too carefully controlled and restricted. Movement provides others with information about us, information which is more likely to provoke a favourable response. Even unattractive people can appear attractive if they have lively and expressive faces. Many comedians are ugly or have odd-looking faces, yet their faces are usually so expressive that their ugliness almost becomes a kind of beauty.

Head movements, especially nods, can help to keep an encounter progressing smoothly and so they, too, should be encouraged. The more you allow, and even encourage, other people to talk, the more they will like you. Not that you should content yourself with being a permanent listener, simply that you should seek to share the floor, as it were, and avoid hogging it.

Gestures should be open and expressive, but not to the point of being contrived and affected. Just let them flow as a natural accompaniment both to the rest of your body language and to what you say. Avoid defensive, barrier gestures. Palm up or palm outward gestures are especially useful to encourage. On the other hand, it is worth noting that high-status individuals exhibit low peripheral movement in the form of few gestures and few changes in posture. Once again, it is a question of judging what is most appropriate in the circumstances.

Posture should be upright with forward lean when trying to convey active interest and involvement. But there are times when an asymmetrical leaning back will help to keep the atmosphere informal and relaxed. Stooping and slouching should always be avoided as these will almost always give an impression of lack of interest or other negative feelings.

Proximity should be encouraged. In our Western culture we tend to distance ourselves rather more than in many other cultures, so there can be several advantages in allowing closeness. We can always soften any stress produced by this by adopting an indirect orientation. When we are alone it is worth remembering that reflective thought is encouraged more by a horizontal orientation than a vertical one.

Bodily contact should be encouraged where it will not lead to embarrassment. Handshakes, arm pats, shoulder pats, arm round shoulders and guiding hands on the arm or back may be the best ones to start with. But, as we said, care needs to be exercised here and progress in using bodily contact should be dictated by what others find appropriate. It is more a question of following others' initiatives rather than taking too much of a lead.

Appearance and physique should be changed where you can see that this will bring about improvements. Experimenting with clothing can often reveal new ways of dressing which produce a more favourable response from others. Since a high value has been placed upon slimness in our society, overweight people might seriously consider either slimming down or at least dressing in ways which disguise the excess flesh.

Timing and synchronization are based on such subtle signals that it takes a good deal of time and effort to refine them. Nevertheless, it is worth working to improve them. Perhaps the best way is to observe carefully those people you can identify as having a particularly acute sense of timing and who are able to synchronize with others with seeming perfection.

Non-verbal aspects of speech provide an area in which, once you are aware of the characteristics of your own speech – perhaps by listening to a tape of yourself – you can exercise some control. Avoid speaking too loudly with too harsh a tone. Avoid speaking too rapidly and using 'umms', 'ers', and 'ahs' wherever you can. Aim to maintain as uninterrupted a flow of speech as possible, without seeming too polished and glib.

Above all, you should remember that body language is only one communication skill. It is limited in the amount and range of information it can convey and is most suited to portraying emotions and attitudes. But because it does also have a vital role in supporting (or contradicting) verbal communication it needs to be developed in the same way as other communication skills. Keep an eye on your own and other people's body language, practise the instruction and guidance offered in this book, read other books on body language and you should find that, as your skill in using it continues to improve, your enjoyment and satisfaction in interacting with other people grows accordingly. You will be taking important steps in the development of your full potential and will be helping others in the achievement of the highest objectives to which humankind can aspire, the growth of human understanding and the promotion of truly effective interpersonal communication.

FURTHER READING

In research terms, in spite of the fact that some research was done over a hundred years ago, body language (or non-verbal communication, as researchers usually call it) is still a very young subject. Although a great deal of research has been done in the last thirty years, much remains to be done. Nevertheless, you will, if you wish to pursue your interest in body language, find it useful to read some of the books below.

Argyle, M. (1972) *The Psychology of Interpersonal Behaviour*, Penguin.

Argyle, M. (1975) *Bodily Communication*, Methuen.

Axtell, R.E. (1998) *Gestures: The Do's and Don'ts of Body Language Around the World*, Wiley.

Birdwhistell, R. (1973) *Kinesics and Context*, Penguin.

Blake, A. (1997) *Body Language: The Meaning of Modern Sport*, Lawrence & Wishart.

Caro, M. (1994) *The Body Language of Poker*, Carol Publishing Corporation.

Cook, M. & McHenry, R. (1978) *Sexual Attraction*, Pergamon.

Clayton, P. (1999) *Body Language: A Visual Guide*, Newleaf.

Cohen, D. (1999) *Body Language in Relationships*, Sheldon Press.

Cundiff, M. (1972) *Kinesics*, Parker Publishing Co (USA).

Darwin, C. (1865, republished 1965) *Expression of the Emotions in Man and Animals*, University of Chicago Press.

Diagram Group (1999) *Body Language*, Harper Collins.

Duckman, D., Rozelle, R.M. & Baxter, J.C. (1982) *Nonverbal Communication*, Sage Publications.

Early, G. (ed.) (1998) *Body Language: Writers on Sport*, Graywolf Press.

Ekman, P. & Friesen, W.V. (1975) *Unmasking the Face*, Prentice-Hall.

Fast, J. (1971) *Body Language*, Pan Books.

Hall, E.T. (1959) *The Silent Language*, Doubleday.

Hall, J.W. (1999) *Body Language*, Harper Collins.

Harrison, R. (1974) *Beyond Words*, Prentice-Hall.

Hess, E.H. (1975) *The Tell-Tale Eye*, Van Nostrand Reinhold.

Jourard, S. (1971) *Self-disclosure*, Wiley.

Kleinke, C. (1975) *First Impressions*, Prentice-Hall.

Knapp, M.L. (1972) *Nonverbal Communication in Human Interaction*, Holt, Rinehart & Winston.

Korte, B. (1998) *Body Language in Literature*, University of Toronto Press.

Lamb, W. (1965) *Posture and Gesture*, Duckworth.

Lewis, D. (1996) *The Body Language of Children*, Souvenir Press.

Lovitt, J. (1996) *Body Language*, Lillenas Publishing.

Matthews, R.O. (1990) *Signs and Symbols: Body Language*, Wayland.

Mehrabian, A. (1971) *Silent Messages*, Wadsworth.

Mehrabian, A. (1972) *Nonverbal Communication*, Aldine Atherton.

Morris, D. (1977) *Manwatching*, Cape.

Morris, D. (1979) *Gestures*, Cape.

Neill, S. & Caswell, C. (1993) *Body Language for Competent Teachers*, Routledge.

Nierenberg, G.I. & Calero, H.H. (1973) *How To Read A Person Like A Book*, Hanau.

Quilliam, S. (1995) *Body Language Secrets for Success at Work*, Thorsons.

Robson, P. (1998) *Body Language*, F. Watts.

Rosenthal, R. (ed) (1979) *Skill in Nonverbal Communication Individual Differences*, Oelgeschlager, Gunn & Ham.

Ruesch, J. & Kees, W. (1956) *Nonverbal Communication*, University of California Press.

Ruthrof, H. (1998) *The Body in Language*, Cassell.

Scheften, A.E. (1972) *Body Language and Social Order*, Prentice-Hall.

Sommer, R. (1969) *Personal Space*, Prentice-Hall.

Wiemann, J.M. & Harrison, R.P. (1983) *Nonverbal Interaction*, Sage Publications.

Wilson, G. & McLaughlin, C. (1996) *Winning With Body Language*, Bloomsbury.

Wilson, G. & Nias, D. (1976) *Love's Mysteries*, Open Books.

Zunin, L. (1972) *Contact: The First Four Minutes*, Talmy Franklin.

INDEX

Other related titles

 TEACH YOURSELF

DREAM INTERPRETATION

LEILA BRIGHT

What do our dreams mean? Throughout recorded history, this question has fascinated people from all over the world. *Teach Yourself Dream Interpretation* is a complete handbook, simple, practical and easy to use, suggesting a host of possible answers. Dreams can serve as guides to the inner-self, and to relationships, health and career success.

This book explains how to benefit from the power of dreams by:

- recalling dreams vividly and distinguishing significant from insignificant dreams
- learning to work with symbols to gain insight into the messages hidden in dreams
- appreciating the role played by specific types of dream – prophetic, anxiety, sexual, etc.
- harnessing the power of lucid and mutual dreaming
- learning to generate dreams to help solve specific problems.

It includes case studies and sample entries from dream diaries as well as a comprehensive, quick-reference A–Z of the meaning of symbols – from abyss to zoo, fog to sunshine, bereavement to birth, plus hundreds of others in between.

Leila Bright is a long-time student of metaphysical issues and has written on topics as diverse as reincarnation and prediction.

Other related titles

MEDITATION

NAOMI OZANIEC

Meditation is a traditional discipline which has been practised through the ages, and has long been recognized for its spiritual and restorative powers.

Teach Yourself Meditation introduces the theory and practice of meditation in a direct and simple manner. The book includes a variety of appoaches, and compares the methods and goals of both Eastern and Western systems. With its holistic view of life, meditation can help you to gain a new perspective for the future.

Naomi Ozaniec has studied meditation for over ten years and has written several books on the subject.

Other related titles

 TEACH YOURSELF

VISUALIZATION

PAULINE WILLS

Visualization, the carrying of a clear visual image in the mind, has long been accepted in the East as playing an important role in balancing and maintaining the mind-body-spirit relationship.

This book will show you how to practise the techniques, using simple, clearly illustrated exercises, to relieve stress, alleviate specific health problems and increase your sense of well-being – in your personal relationships, at work, and in all aspects of your everyday life. The book includes a selection of mandalas which you can use in your quest for personal growth.

Pauline Wills first trained as a nurse. She subsequently developed an interest in complementary therapies, and now uses visualization alongside a wide range of other treatments. She has written extensively on reflexology and colour therapy.

Other related titles

ZEN
a way of life
CHRISTMAS HUMPHREYS

This well-known introduction to Zen explains and points the way to the experience of Zen, bringing heightened consciousness, spiritual fulfilment and enlightenment.

With this book, Christmas Humphreys, founder of the Buddhist Society, London – now the oldest and largest Buddhist organization in Europe – has made an important contribution to the understanding of Zen. He begins by discussing the basic doctrine of Buddhism and the expanded principles of Mahayana Buddhism. Having described the background to the Zen school of Buddhism, he turns to Zen itself and examines the actual process of self-training towards the Zen experience of Reality.